SPIRIT CHILD

HEALING THE WOUND OF ABORTION

To Aine

with love from Babcha xa

Glastonbury, August 2006.

British Library Cataloguing-in-Publication Data.
A catalogue record for this book is available
from the British Library.

Cover design and book layout
by David Gregson.

Printed and bound by WSOY, Finland.

Published by
Findhorn Press
The Park, Findhorn
Forres IV36 0TZ
Scotland
tel +44 (0)1309 690582/fax 690036
email: thierry@findhorn.org
http://www.findhorn.org/findhornpress/

SPIRIT CHILD

HEALING THE WOUND OF ABORTION

Isabella M. Kirton

FINDHORN
Press

*This book is dedicated
to spirit children everywhere.*

ACKNOWLEDGEMENTS

I would like to acknowledge the protection and guidance that I have received from the Masters, in particular Serapis Bey, Maha Chohan, Lao Tzu and Kwan Yin.

I would like to acknowledge the inspiration and love that I have received from the realm of angels and in particular from my spirit child whose presence I have felt throughout the writing of this book.

I would like to acknowledge the sensitivity and loving support that I have received from my family of friends: Laurie, Rosemary, Pam, Diana, Penny D., Geraldine, Anstice, Cecilia and last but not least Geoffrey, my ex-husband.

I would like to acknowledge the love and acceptance that I have received from my children Alix, Charles and Augustine, always, and in particular throughout the research and writing of this book.

I would like to acknowledge the generosity of spirit of the women who contributed to this book and who walked with me: Clare, Colette, my osteopath, Betty, Melanie, Elizabeth, Maggie and Francoise.

I would like to acknowledge the vision and trust that I have received from Karin and Thierry Bogliolo, Sandra Kramer's skilful editing and David Gregson's beautiful cover design. It has been a privilege to work with Findhorn Press.

I would like to acknowledge the generous help that I received from Susan Mears and from the late Ian Gordon-Brown while this book was in the process of manifestation.

I would like to acknowledge two men from whom I have learnt hard, hard lessons: Geoffrey, the father of my three children, who by leaving home catapulted me into my journey into the unknown, and Vincent, the father of my spirit child, whose short-lived presence in my life ensured that I remained on that journey.

And, finally, I would like to acknowledge Chile, a country where I have felt a deep and strong earth connection. Without this earth connection I doubt whether I would have had the courage and the energy to manifest this vision.

Thank you all.

FOREWORD

This sensitively written and timely book, on an emotive subject that is still taboo to many people, will be welcomed by any woman who has been through a pregnancy termination or a miscarriage.

Women who have a termination experience a myriad of emotions ranging from relief to grief, guilt, loss and a sense of emptiness and abandonment. There is nothing to prepare one for these feelings. Although it is often a consciously taken decision, the termination of a pregnancy, just like a miscarriage, can cause a woman to feel like a victim — disempowered. Whatever the reason for ending a life miraculously conceived within a woman's body, the female psyche remains prepared for the whole magical process of birth. Emotionally and physically — especially hormonally — the body still appears to be in the pregnant state. It is as if the switch has not been switched off, which perhaps explains why many women are highly sensitive and emotional at the time when they would have given birth, often being over-whelmed by sudden tears at the sight of a newborn baby in a pram.

Traditionally, women in indigenous cultures were and still are much closer to nature and in tune with the rhythms and cycles of Mother Earth. They are more in touch with their bodies and the miracle of the birthing process and are able to connect easily with the realms of spirit. Many women in our society too are now opening up to these subtle dimensions, another form of reality, and report hearing their child talking to them or even seeing their child in spirit form.

Spirit Child beautifully and movingly tells the story of one woman's unique journey and search for self-discovery and her process of emotional and spiritual healing through the inner relationship she develops with her child. I am delighted to have been part of that process through flower remedies.

Many women will be able to identify with this story and it will become a catalyst and an empowering aid to their own self-healing process. Out of loss and grief rises a positive experience of hope and joy as women make contact with their spirit children and become at peace with them. And as Isabella Kirton spells out in this book, these spirit children come to us as our teachers to remind us of our connection to spirit and our own spirituality.

Clare G. Harvey
Middle Piccadilly, 1998

Clare G. Harvey is a Flower Essence consultant at The Hale Clinic and Middle Piccadilly Natural Healing Centre and co-author of *The Encyclopaedia of Flower Remedies* and *Vibrational Healing*.

INTRODUCTION

In my early forties I had an abortion — a step that many women of all ages feel they have to take. The purpose of this book is to share with others my experience of that act and in particular the relationship that developed between my unborn child and myself. By accepting and honouring this relationship I have been able to heal myself of the wound created by my abortion.

I was already the mother of three children. I was not in a relationship. Although unaware of it at the time, I now believe with the wisdom of hindsight that I went through this experience so I could one day write about it.

I had a relationship with my child prior to the abortion. I thought the abortion would sever this contact, but in fact I felt myself still to be pregnant. Part of this book describes those months between the abortion and the time when the child would have been born. At that time I had a very vivid and physical experience of giving birth — a process easy to identify from the previous births in my life. This event opened me up to a different level of consciousness and I spent the following three days having out-of-body experiences. I felt I was cracking up. Some people may call it having a nervous breakdown.

Here I tell the story of my long journey towards healing which involved integrating into my everyday life all the different experiences I had had and accepting them as part of my learning in this incarnation. I describe the times when my child in spirit came to me in my dreams and in my waking imagination and how she nourished our relationship by the things she taught me.

Readers may find some of the experiences far-fetched. Indeed I found them so myself. Part of the learning for me *was* to learn to approach these experiences from a different perspective and accept that the act of abortion was more complex than I had imagined. I had thought it would simply happen and then I could get on with my life, but it wasn't going to be like that. I could no longer get on with my life as I knew it. The challenges posed by the world that opened up to me after the 'birth' of my child have completely transformed my life as I have learnt to let the intuitive and spiritual side of myself develop and grow.

I feel that now is the moment to share this knowledge. I have already started this work in a small way within the groups I run. The response I have had to the material I have talked about has been overwhelming. Many, many women and individuals who work in the caring professions know that these experiences not only happen but in some cases have even happened to them. It is simply that the story has never been told.

PROLOGUE

"I was conceived on a wet and cold Friday afternoon.
I had been waiting to come to Isabella for some time but she was
always very careful not to take any risks.
That Friday afternoon, however, she was a little careless.
I saw my opportunity and I slipped through into the physical
world once again.
I needed just a touch of life and she needed to learn
what I could teach her. She was ready for me."

—Helena Rose

CHAPTER ONE

My abortion, as it turned out, was not the end of my pregnancy. I didn't know it for another six months and six days — months and days when I carried my baby in every way except biologically. At the time I came home, cooked the supper and went to bed, relieved that the experience was, so I thought, behind me.

That night I had no idea that for the next few months I would regularly wonder whether I was going mad. I soon began to experience bouts of uncontrollable weeping that would sweep over me, unpredictable moods that accompanied me everywhere and furious outbursts of anger that felt as powerful and destructive as volcanic eruptions. At other times I just wanted to be alone and far away. Away from people, even those that I loved; away from my work; away from all the demands of my life. I wanted to bury myself in the dark, healing womb of Mother Earth and go to sleep. I wanted to sleep a peaceful sleep until it was all over and I could wake up healed and myself again.

Nobody had told me it would be like this. All they said was, "Oh, it's just a few minutes under a light anaesthetic and you might feel a little bit sick when you come round." Nobody mentioned that I might feel devastated, that it would take time to recover, that I should be gentle with myself — that I might still feel pregnant.

I didn't dare talk to anyone about the experiences I was going through. I cried in private, alone. I hardly slept at night; vivid dreams woke me at three in the morning. More often than not the dreams and images were terrifying and kept me awake for the few hours remaining until dawn.

One of the recurring dreams I had at the time was that I was still pregnant. I would wake, sweating with fear at the prospect of going through another abortion. Every month, imagining that my period was late, I would go out and buy the Predictor set and test myself. At a rational, logical level, I knew I was not pregnant. At a rational, logical level I knew that my behaviour was bizarre. But this was not a rational or logical time for me.

I quickly learnt that to survive I needed to focus on practical activities. During the day I would go about my work, run my practice, go to Sainsbury's, drive my children and their friends to school, and pick them up at the end of the day. I would force myself to keep busy: the dog went for ten times as many walks as usual, for the first and last time the washing and ironing were always up to date and the bills were paid on time as I ruthlessly applied myself to these activities. In fact the structure and hard work of my life as a single working mother with three teenage children supported me through those months. It was at night that I felt haunted. It was at night that I was alone. This was when my imagination took over and I thought I was going insane. I dreaded the nights during those months. I would tell myself that if I was pregnant I could always have another abortion. And that is when the tears would flow and I would weep, passionately, hysterically. I would weep as if my heart was breaking.

I eventually talked to someone who suggested that I should go back into therapy. But I knew that this was not a subject I was ready to talk about. In some ways the experience I was going through was completely non-verbal. It had a life of its own in the language of symbols and dreams and body sensations. Words simply couldn't capture the depth of the experience. How could I begin to explain to someone that I felt I was still pregnant? How could I explain to anybody that I *knew* I was still pregnant even though I had had my foetus aborted? Even though I knew I was not getting fatter. Even though I knew that my breasts had resumed their normal size and no longer ached. I couldn't begin to do that. So, although the suggestion of therapy had been offered in good faith, I found it useless.

The father of my little foetus, to whom I talked occasionally, was equally unhelpful.

"Shouldn't you be over it by now?" he would say impatiently. "You're taking a long time to get over it!"

I felt deeply wounded by his words, although I knew that he only spoke impatiently because he too had been upset by the experience and felt powerless to do anything to help me. I was beyond help. I was beyond reach in those months as I went about my daily tasks. I wondered then and still do now whether my children were aware of anything different going on? I have never asked them.

Spring arrived and I hardly noticed. I took on more responsibility at work. It helped me to fill my time so that I wouldn't have a free moment during which my inner world could intrude into my consciousness. I had enough free time during the night hours when my inner world took centre stage.

My most vivid image I called 'The Black Hole'. I wrote about it endlessly in my journal. The first time the black hole came to me, I was terrified. I stood on the outside of it and looked at this deep blackness that stretched ahead of me, feeling as if I would fall into the nothingness of the night and disappear. Night after night the black hole returned to haunt me, like an uninvited guest in my dreams. What could I say to it to make it go away? So that I would be left on my own, undisturbed?

There was nothing I could say and no one I could say it to.

Night after night I awoke in terror, sweating and shivering, rigid with fear as the black hole lay sprawling in front of me. In my mind, I couldn't go into it. My fantasy was that I wouldn't be able to see and, as I was short-sighted anyway, the fear of not being able to see was vivid. I had a sense that I would drown in the blackness of it. I would suffocate in the airlessness of it. I would be lost in the nothingness of it.

Every night I dreaded going to sleep, knowing that in a few hours I would wake up sweating and shivering when my uninvited guest appeared. I would prepare carefully for bed, taking a glass of water to have beside me. I would put four drops of Rescue Remedy into it. I would look up at the night sky through my bedroom window and pray to whomever was out there: "Please, not tonight. Please, please, please let me sleep. Let me sleep, just for one night."

Nobody heard me. There was nobody out there to care. I awoke shivering and sweating again and again and again.

Then one night something was different. One night I approached the blackness slowly, hesitantly. I had reached the point where I felt that to enter it could no longer be any worse than what I was experiencing while I remained outside of it.

I stood on the edge and couldn't see. I stood on the edge and let myself be cooled and soothed by the velvety blackness of it. I felt the moist air and was calmed by it. I reached out into the nothingness with my hand and saw my hand disappear.

The heat and fire of my terror calmed down. The black smoothness soothed my skin and I stepped forward into the black hole. The darkness enveloped me. I floated in the nothingness of it. For a moment I wondered whether I would return to my bed to meet another day. Was I dying? I looked up and saw stars in the blackness, the night blackness of the hole. Stars, shining and bright. And then I knew I was alive.

I had not died, I lived. Tears poured down my cheeks as I allowed my body to be suspended inside the black hole. I had found the deep, healing place inside the womb of Mother Earth that I had been seeking. I had found it in my black hole, which at first had seemed so terrifying and hostile but then had become my friend.

Then, only then, did I sleep.

I slept peacefully and awoke refreshed for another day. I awoke feeling like a new blade of grass fresh with dew after a night of storms.

After that, my nights were tolerable. The black hole returned to visit me but I knew now that I could walk into it and that by doing so I would regain my sense of peace and my terror would be soothed. In fact there were nights when I welcomed my guest. I began to look forward to the feelings of deep, deep peace which the black hole now engendered in me and which I could carry into my days which were getting busier and busier.

I still felt pregnant but I now accepted the feelings and sensations that had become a part of me. I started to review my life and realised that I had taken on too much, that I needed to cut back on my work.

Summer had arrived. The sun is very important to me as a South American and it was shining most days. I flourish and flower when the sun shines. I feel connected to my vital core. The buddleia was out in the garden and the warm scent of it pleased me. I loved watching the butterflies hovering over it.

There was one particularly beautiful evening that stands out vividly. The moon was full — a full moon in Capricorn. The day had been a peerless one, the summer breezes warm and gentle, the air hot. I felt as if I was beginning to heal.

"I'm getting over it," I thought to myself. "I'm beginning to be myself again." I was now eight months pregnant and there was nothing physical to show for it. I began to accept that I was no longer carrying a foetus.

I began to drift and dream in the summer days. The holidays had started and there were children in the streets during the days. Their laughter, language, energy and enthusiasm delighted me.

And then one beautiful July morning I awoke early. Lying in bed, hearing the birds calling out to each other, in that dreamy state before one opens one's eyes, I suddenly saw her.

CHAPTER TWO

It was a warm, summer's dawn. The birds were singing in the trees outside my bedroom window. I could see the sun, glowing and hot, just rising over the rooftops of the houses opposite.

I lay in my bed, in my east-facing bedroom, with my eyes closed. I lay in my bed luxuriating in the glory of this new day. In the brilliance of the sun. In the songs of the birds. I lay in my bed, dozing quietly.

I had to teach that day and for the two days following. I was doing an 'Introduction to Counselling' course. I always enjoyed teaching the introductory modules. The people who participated in them were at a moment of choice in their lives. Were they going to train to become counsellors? Were they going to train in the person-centred approach? Were they going to train at this Institute? Did they have the courage to make the sort of far-reaching changes in their lives that embarking on a counselling course would entail? We, the tutors, always said that counselling training carried a government health warning! Only enter the course if you are ready to be fundamentally changed by the experience. I found it a privilege and a pleasure to accompany the students for these particular days. They were at a crossroads in their lives with all the potential and all the misgivings that such opportunities present.

So I was looking forward to the next three days. I had begun to feel that the past was finally behind me. That I could move on from my abortion. That life was beginning, finally, to regain some semblance of normality. I was starting to enjoy the present moment. Life seemed to beckon me on this beautiful summer's day.

I lay there, blissfully unaware of the crossroads I myself had reached. Blissfully unaware that my life was about to change direction dramatically. Unaware of the entrance into my life of my fourth child. I lay there, my eyes closed, dozing and dreaming in the early morning summer sunshine.

And then she came into view. A small bundle of baby. She stayed there, in my view. A small bundle of baby. A delicious small bundle of a baby. With my eyes still closed, I could see her clearly. The image was sharp and clear.

I opened my eyes and she was gone. I was still in my bedroom, in my east-facing bedroom with the early morning sun pouring through the crack in the closed curtains. The birds were still singing outside and I knew that I would soon be on my way.

I thought I would close my eyes again. Would she still be there? I took a deep breath and allowed my eyelids to fall shut slowly. She was still there, in my mind's eye. A beautiful, sleeping baby girl.

I opened my eyes again. I was still in my bedroom. It was still a morning in July. I was still going to teach and the birds were still singing. I began to wonder what was going on.

Who was this baby? Why was she there? Why did she appear every time I closed my eyes? How did she get there — or rather, here? I couldn't understand. The image of this baby, this newborn baby, was so vivid, so real, so clear. It didn't fade or change. It was simply there, every time I closed my eyes.

I decided to close my eyes quite deliberately this time. "I will close them and really observe her," I told myself.

So I closed my eyes and, yes, there she was again.

She was definitely newborn. Definitely premature by two or three weeks. I could tell that by the thinness of her legs. They hadn't had time to fill out as babies do in the last two or three weeks of pregnancy. I had carried three babies to full term and so was very familiar with how they should look. "This one has been born early," I thought.

Her eyes were tightly closed. Her hair, peeping out from under a white embroidered cotton bonnet was black. Black,

black, black. "That's strange," I thought. "I had black hair when I was born but none of my other children did."

Other children? What did I mean by 'other children'? That implied that this was also my child. But she couldn't be. How could she be my child? I returned to observing her, now even more puzzled and bewildered.

She was wearing a little white cotton dress embroidered with the same pattern that was on her bonnet — lambs frisking in a field of green grass. The sun was round and yellow. There was a pond, stitched in blue, surrounded by blades of green grass. Ducks were swimming on the pond. Ducks with their ducklings swimming behind them.

Someone had made this dress with a great deal of love. What care had gone into the detail of the workmanship! The joy of the lambs in the spring sunshine. The paddling around of the ducklings. Every stitch had been an act of love. I could see that. Who had made this dress?

I wanted to reach out and touch her. Touch her dress; touch her fingers and face; touch her little knees peeking out from beneath the dress. But I didn't. I simply watched her as she lay there, peacefully sleeping. Her face was pink, pale pink. Her legs were also pink, a darker pink. And they were long, and thin. She was wearing little white woollen bootees on her feet, tied with a white satin ribbon. She was adorable. I wanted to cuddle her. I wanted to rock her in my arms and sing to her. I wanted to hold her to my heart. She reminded me of a doll that I had had as a child.

But this was no doll. I could see that. She was breathing lightly and every now and again she would give a small sigh and moisten her lips. I wondered again why this baby had appeared to me. Why had she come, out of the blue, at this moment in time? Why had she come on this July morning? Why had she chosen to appear to me? I never thought, at that moment, of asking her these questions directly. I was full of questions and maybe didn't yet want to have any answers.

I knew it was time to get up and go to work. I had a busy three days ahead of me. I had asked someone to work with me and I needed time with my colleague to go over her role in the group. I opened my eyes and left the baby girl behind, or so I thought. I got up, showered and dressed and drove to the Institute.

It was lunchtime when I started to feel unwell. I didn't think much of it at first; just a slight nausea and stomach cramps. "It will pass," I said to myself as I planned the afternoon's activities with my colleague. But I was glad she was there with me.

The pain in my stomach started just after the lunch break. I had already been feeling a little dizzy over lunch. The pain had a strange character. It came and went. It was intense and it faded away. While I was free of pain I was fine and was able to listen and talk and teach, but when it returned I was in too much agony to do anything. As the early afternoon progressed I became aware that the pains in my stomach were becoming more severe and were coming more regularly — every twenty minutes or so. My nausea was getting worse. The pains became more like severe cramps.

I couldn't think what was the matter with me. Had I eaten something that had disagreed with me the night before? Was I contracting some infection? I have always believed in a mind-body connection and when my body speaks I wonder what is going on at other levels. The particularly curious thing was that I have always felt very healthy when I am running a module. I sometimes get ill afterwards and have always put that down to my body recovering from a very intense and emotional three days. This was definitely a first for me.

I realised that I would have to go home. I spoke to my colleague and although she was not a senior trainer she felt able to run the last slot of the afternoon on her own. I left the Institute wondering whether I would make it home at all. I could hardly focus on driving. The nausea swept over me in waves. The cramps in my stomach... "This pain isn't in my stomach," I thought. "It feels as if it's in my womb. It feels like a very severe period pain." I recollected that my period had arrived three weeks late the last time and that my periods had been quite haphazard for several months, contributing to my sense of being pregnant. Could these cramps have

anything to do with that? I decided I couldn't thi
at that moment. I didn't want to think about it. I j
to get home, stretch out on my bed and forget l
feeling, how very wretched I was feeling. I thought, ..i i can
just get home, I'll be better."

On arriving home, I went straight to my bedroom and collapsed onto my bed, which I had left so cheerfully earlier that day. The house was empty. The children were away for the weekend with their father. The pains in my womb were coming with increasing regularity now. There was no doubt in my mind that they were centred in my womb. They felt like intense period pains. When they came, I was bent double with the pain. Then they would ebb away and I would feel relieved.

After a while I began to notice a pattern emerging. A wave of pain. A build up, a peak and then it would pass. This continued for hour after hour. Sometime in the evening I noticed that the gap between the contractions...

"The WHAT?" I gasped, astonished at the thought that had entered my mind.

But, yes, I did mean contractions because that is what they reminded me of. Now that the thought had entered my mind I couldn't rid myself of it and the similarity to the labour pains that I had experienced three times before was very clear to me. I was in labour and the contractions were coming more frequently now.

But how could I be? What did it mean? I remembered how I had felt in the afternoon: the periods of time, between the agonising spasms, when I had felt fine. But now the waves of pain merged into each other with little or no space between them. I couldn't believe what I was experiencing and I felt frightened, very frightened.

I knew now that I was in labour. In labour with my fourth child, the one I had aborted just over six months ago. She would have been born, had she lived, in about three weeks' time. She was arriving early, this child that I had chosen not to have on the earth plane. I had chosen to terminate her life in a physical body. But she was arriving anyway. She was arriving in spirit. She was being born to me in spirit through my body. How was I so sure of this? It was because I carried within me an ancient feminine wisdom that rose up from the depths of my being to help me at this time. What would be the end of it all? I knew that no physical child could be born.

I didn't want to think about how it would all end. I just knew that I was in labour. And I knew that I needed to live through the experience second by second. My child was being born, although I would never see her or hold her or smell her or touch her. She was coming to me in spirit and I had no idea why she had chosen to do so.

Late that night, the pains reached a crescendo. There was a roaring in my ears, a deep cry from my heart and soul, a yearning to give birth, to push. To push as I had already done three times before with my other children. I pushed and pushed, holding on to my pillow as my body went into a final spasm before, finally, I was still.

I lay on my bed, weeping, sobbing, exhausted. I felt that my heart would break. I would never hold her in my arms but I knew that she was alive. I could feel her presence in the room with me. I felt surrounded by love and by a loving presence. Slowly I stopped weeping. I just lay there in my east-facing bedroom, feeling tranquil and at peace. Feeling as if I was being rocked by Mother Earth. The darkness of my room reminded me of the black hole and I could feel again the velvety softness of it. I was being held in the womb of the Mother.

I decided to call her Helena Rose. I don't know why. Rose was the name given to my great-grandmother's twin sister. I have always felt a strong connection with my great-grandmother. Calling my baby Rose seemed a good idea. Later that summer, while walking in a field in St. Just in Cornwall, I came across a chapel dedicated to St. Helena — a very ancient monument overlooking the sea.

As I lay in my bed that night, I had no idea that Helena Rose was going to change my life. I had no idea of the events that would flow and race through my life, churning up the depths, dredging the bottom of my unconscious. I had no idea of any of it.

I didn't know that she would visit me occasionally and unexpectedly, nor that she would become as real to me as my three living children. It took me a long time to accept and understand that she was living too. Only not on this side. On the other side, the unseen side. I would have to learn about travelling to the other side, in the process shedding many of the ways I had adopted in order to survive my physical existence. I would have to remember how I, too, could journey back and forth and bring what I learnt from one side to the other.

In my attempt to survive on Earth, I had buried much of what I knew of the spirit side. My mother tells of how she used to tease me for 'talking to spirits'. The story in the family goes that one day, when I was about five years old, I was chatting away, holding onto my mother's hand. My mother asked me: "Who are you talking to, Isabella?" I responded, "Oh! All these people; they won't leave me alone. They are always telling me things. I wish they would go away and leave me alone."

And of course they had. They had gone away and left me alone, except in my dream life and in the occasional stirring of memories that whispered to me: "You are not alone." These memories reminded me that there is a place I come from that I call 'home'. I know it isn't any physical place. The nearest I have come to finding it is when I have travelled in the Andes in central Chile. I feel I have always known it is there but I had forgotten about its existence. Now the feelings I was having, lying in my bed, reminded me of this place I called home. I had a sense of being surrounded by unconditional love, a sense of weightlessness and warmth, and I could feel the golden light that invaded my room while I lay there with my eyes closed.

I thought back to the early morning of that day and I remembered how I had gazed at her. My spirit child. I had gazed and gazed at her. I knew now that she was my child, the child that I had aborted. I had only aborted her body, not her spirit. Her spirit was here with me now. Reaching out to me, lovingly, divinely. Reaching out to me, for me. Did I want to let her into my life? Would I know how to do that? And what would it mean?

I had no doubt in my mind that this was an experience I could never tell anybody about. This was a private, private matter. I closed my eyes. She was there again. Just as she had been in the early morning. Just as she would be, time after time, even to the present moment. Just as she would be whenever I called her to me. But I didn't know that yet.

At that moment I simply gazed at her, knowing that she was there. I gazed at her miniature features; at her black hair sticking out from under her cotton bonnet. I gazed at her long arms and slim fingers. I gazed at her long legs and tiny, tiny feet. She was precious to behold: soft, pink, newborn and magical. A magical child. And she would bring magic back into my life, although as a well-behaved adult I would have to learn, slowly and painfully, how to listen to her and learn from her.

I would have to learn how to receive the joys that she would offer me. I would have to learn about magic all over again. I would have to learn the lesson of listening to my heart. I had known about magic, once; I had been a magical child myself, once, before I had had to pretend to forget.

CHAPTER THREE

I feel deep, deep as the sea, deep as the ocean. The rocks at the mouth of the bay jut out into the sea. I see a child dive into the sea's depth. I am in the sea, under the blue green water, and I receive the child, the boy child, into my arms.

I rise above the water, above the waves, and I see the man swimming, out swimming, out to find his child, and I hold him up, up out of the water. This bonny, bonny child who has dived deep into the sea. I have the power to return him or to keep him.

He reminds me of a child I once had when I too lived out on the land. In those days when I lived out on the land, when I felt like a fish out of water and I needed, yearned, to return to my own kind. I yearned to return to the depths of living in the sea, in the deep of the ocean.

How do you live in the deep of the land?

I once asked that question, many, many years ago when I lived out on the land. Where can I feel my depth, my deepness, on the land? I go into the forests and I smell the earth, I go out into the rain and I smell the rain. I drench myself in the rain until I become of the rain, until I am the rain itself.

I do the same in the forests. I submerge myself in the woods, in the trees, in the moistness of the leaves fallen on the forest floor, and I become the moistness of the leaves, I become the leaves on the forest floor. I feel the stillness inside me. I start to feel as if I am one with the trees. And then I know that I am one with the trees; and that I have become the tree.

How can I talk to others about this? Who will understand my deepness, my oneness with all living things? But particularly with the rain and the trees? Who can I call on to share with me this passion and colour and power and depth? Who will not run away from me?

I am not frightening to you. I will not threaten you. I simply want to talk to you about these feelings that are a part of me, inside me. How can I make you understand? Who will not be scared of me? Who will not laugh at me? Who will say, "I too know the feeling of being one with the tree and one with the rain"? I search for my beloved and I cannot find him on the land or on the sea. I cannot find him and he does not come to me when I call. He does not come to me.

Shall I find him in the sea?

I turn to the sea. I walk into the ocean and then I realise that I am also of the ocean. I am of the ocean and I am of the rain. I have been a cloud on the mountain top and I have filled the rivers that flow down from the mountain. Who will believe me when I tell them? Who will not call me mad? Insane? Deranged?

I am one with all living things. And then I understand. I know God. He is in me and I am in Him. He is a part of all living things and all living things are a part of Him. This is the mystery and it is no longer a mystery.

I understand. I have crossed the threshold and I live in the spirit world again, connected with all things. The rain, the trees, the ocean and even the child that has dived deep into the sea. I pick him up and hold him up for the man to see. He is a fair child, about five years old. What was he looking for in the sea?

And then I remember my child. My child who has come to look for me in the sea. I weep and I hold him. My love, my child, I am also a part of you and you are a part of me. I am also a human.

I ask God, "Let my child's life be easier than mine. Let him know all these things and take them for granted. Let him know that to be a part of all living things is a part of our heritage. It is a gift open to all of us. It is a gift that only requires us to awaken our hearts and have eyes to see and ears to listen. Let him, let all of you who read this, claim your birthright."

Where have we lost this gift? Why have we spurned it?

What have we wanted to put in its place? And has that nourished us? No, NO!

I have searched for my love and I have not found him and he has not found me. Has he searched for me? Does he also have a hunger for me as I have a hunger for him? I know that he is close. I can feel him out there, waiting, waiting... waiting for what?

"I am not ready yet," he says to me through the wind, through the rain, through the forests, through the leaves of the trees. "I am not ready yet for you. One day I will come to you when I am ready. In the meantime do not let your light go out. I need it. We all need it in this dark world.

"We need the Light that you hold inside you. The stillness that is a part of you, the peace that you share with us all, the peace of God that you have allowed yourself to receive, that you know how to let into your heart — that we have all forgotten how to allow into our hearts. Our lives have gone on, day after day, unquestioning, unfaithful and unchanged in their darkness.

"Wait for me and I will come to you; but not now, it is not the time and it is not the place. When the time and the place are ready, I will come and you will know me and I will know you and we will love together."

I heard my love speak to me through the wind and the rain and the leaves of the forest. I heard my love speak to me from the cloud at the top of the mountain and from the rivers that flow down the mountain. I heard my love.

Strident, harsh, shrill was the sound that brought me back to consciousness. It was the telephone ringing. It rang and rang through the empty house. For a moment I couldn't remember where I was. Where was the telephone? Why couldn't someone answer it? It went on and on. The sound of its bell pounded through my head, bringing me back to the here and now. Slowly I struggled to reach over to the receiver, to see who was calling. Slowly I lifted it. The caller had rung off.

I put the telephone down, feeling sick and dizzy. My body felt heavy, drugged. Had I been dreaming? Where had I been? I knew I had been somewhere, somewhere beautiful, full of

Light, out of this world. But now I felt split up, fragmented.

There was a heavy part of me, of my body it seemed. This heavy part of me felt exhausted and drained. I thought back to the events of the previous day but found them incomprehensible. I couldn't make sense of things. My mind was shrouded in thick fog.

And there was also another part of me. A part which felt light and translucent. This part of me was supremely happy: "I feel full of light," that part of me said. "I feel part of the light. I can float. I'm in touch with all Creation. I'm a part of the Living God. I have been home."

The heavy part of me could hardly move. "Will I ever be able to make it out of bed?" it wondered. "How will I be able to get back to the training group?"

"I will help you," the light part of me answered.

"You? How are you going to help me?" the heavy part groaned in response. "I'm aching in every limb and sore in every muscle of my body."

The light part of me floated about. I could see the heavy part of me lying exhausted on the bed. I knew I could help this heavy part but in order to do so I would need to communicate with it somehow. What to do?

At that moment, the telephone started ringing again. The two parts of me came together in an instant. I reached over to pick up the receiver, fully conscious this time.

"Hello," I said. "Who is it?"

"Isabella? It's me... " It was my colleague on the course. "How are you feeling? I was wondering when you were thinking you might be back?"

"I'll be there by the coffee break," I answered her. "Can you hold the group until then?"

"Yes, yes, of course. But are you all right? You sound odd, somehow, as if you were very far away."

"I'm fine", I replied, for once relieved that English social conventions enabled me to be scarce with the truth.

It was odd how quickly I was able to come to and respond to an ordinary thing like a telephone call. It was odd how quickly the fragmented parts of me were able to come together and function as a whole person again.

This oddity was only the first of many over the next couple of days. It was odd the way that I managed to get dressed and drive into work without any memory of doing so. I felt as if a part of me was on automatic: performing by rote the things that I was so used to doing. I felt as if my body was a shell and that the inside of it was somewhere else. Getting dressed was simply putting things onto the shell; driving the car was simply putting the shell behind the steering wheel and trusting the part of me that had many years' experience of driving to operate it.

The next few days passed and I have hardly any memory of them. I know that I attended the module until the end. I know that I completed the work of the module in a satisfactory manner and that several participants commented on what a 'spiritual experience' it had been for them. I didn't ask them what they meant. I know that I had not looked at my notes and that I was teaching from a different part of me, one that seemed to have knowledge from another dimension, that was linked to some cosmic consciousness I had been unaware of until that moment of my life. Maybe that was what they were referring to.

I know all these things and yet I also don't know them. I was in a very strange place within myself, hardly aware of time and place, of the cycle of days and nights. How would it end? I lived in the moment and as I attempt to write about it all now I struggle to find the words to communicate my experience.

I know that my body continued to do all the things that it needed to do in order to function: eat, sleep, drink, pee and crap. But 'I' was not in it. Not the 'I' as I am used to knowing myself.

I am writing this as if I were at that time two separate people, and in a way that is how I felt. Part of me was an outer shell, functioning normally. And then there was an inner consciousness which was connected to all things and to a feeling of a great Light and lightness of being. This inner consciousness came from inside the shell of me and shone out of it. The shell was simply a casing of some sort. Its purpose was to surround the light and to give it a shape — to give *me* a shape. I had a strange sense that this shell casing was simply my body and that the light that shone out from inside was my spirit. And my spirit was connected to all things. All things had spirit; some spirits had casings just as I did and then there were others who did not. They simply WERE. And they were everywhere around me and with me.

I remember the beauty of the sensations and feelings I had at that time. It seemed as if the world was a most beautiful place, full of colour and light. I remember that everything had a shimmering glow around it, sparkling in the summer sunshine. I knew I was connected to all things and all things were connected to me. I felt as if I were made of light, composed of Light, a Light Being. I shimmered and glowed in the summer sunshine of that July afternoon.

I knew that every thought and every word expressed in the world had a life of its own. Every syllable had its own shape and colour and sound. Every one of them had a birth, a life and a death. The atmosphere was full of these creatures that we humans were creating every second of the day and night. And we didn't even know that we were creating them!

I wondered why we were not all more careful with our words. Couldn't we see the multicoloured ripples that streamed from our mouths as we talked, as we whispered and shouted, gossiped and slandered each other? Blue and black, red and yellow, pink and orange, green and purple, lilac and gold. Ripples that streamed out of the mouths of every living creature on the planet, mixing and mingling and creating patterns of colours in the universe, and affecting the atmosphere around each one of us.

"We really ought to be more careful," I thought. "*I* must be more careful. I didn't know that my words had this impact. Does anyone know?" At one point over those days, I imagined I even saw people's thoughts. I could see them like pictures in my mind that unfolded before me and then drifted away in the summer haze.

I lived through that short time as if in a dreamworld. Time

appeared to expand and become timeless and that timelessness seemed to span the whole world and all of Time. I felt I was hovering above the surface of life experiencing many things that seemed incredible then but less incredible now, five years later. I was in an altered state of consciousness and it was a magical, transcendent experience.

I sat under the silver birches in my garden and heard them whispering to one another, their language so different from our own. The rustle of their leaves on the evening breeze caressed my face. I closed my eyes and felt myself drawn into the little grove to become one with them. I lay down on the damp grass and felt my roots anchoring deep into the earth. Deep, deep my roots went into the earth. Deep, deep into the womb of the Great Mother, into the core of Planet Earth herself. I felt drawn into the earth becoming a part of it. I surrendered to the deep, dark silence of the world before we arrived.

That night, I looked up at the stars outside my bedroom window, my east-facing bedroom window. I reached out my hand to the night sky and caressed the velvety softness of the night, the starlit night. No moon, just stars — like bright points of light, magic light, in the black night sky. I heard the sound of the night sky, the sound of the stars. I reached out my hand to touch a star. My fingers closed over it. The star burned bright in my hand. I could see the glow through my closed fingers. Starlit hand.

I watched in wonder as I released the star into the night sky. It flew across the night, leaving a silver trail through the heavens as it made its way back to its home, its heavenly home. The star still lives. It no longer burns bright in my hand. I let it go, I let it fly free up in the sky. Its brilliant light I can no longer touch. But I know it's there for me and for you.

And so ended my magical, dreamlike days. The next morning I awoke and fell to the ground with a great force. A great force that cracked me up or cracked me open, I don't know which. I just know that I lay split open like a giant coconut dropped from a great height, white flesh exposed, milk dribbling out of me like human blood.

I lay broken and exposed on the ground. I lay on the ground in anguish and despair, writhing in pain and broken-hearted. I lay on the ground wounded, deeply wounded. I remembered my abortion; remembered the decision I had made eight months before to terminate the life of my fourth child, recalling my certainty at the time and wondering whether, after all, I had made a grave mistake.

How could I have predicted the events of the last few days? Could anyone have told me? Could I have been prepared for these strange experiences?

I asked myself these questions as I struggled to come to terms with how I was feeling and what had happened to me. I cast my mind back to the events of nine months before and recalled them in detail once more, hoping that in doing so I might be able to shed some light on my present darkness; that I might find or be given some illumination or enlightenment.

CHAPTER FOUR

As I started to come round over the next few days and find my feet again, my mind was repeatedly drawn to the events of nine months before and the choice I had made to have an abortion. I felt that the roots of the experience I had been through lay in the past. I relived those eight, nine weeks in my mind, remembering every detail of my pregnancy and every reason for deciding to have an abortion.

That decision had been immediate. From the moment that the test confirmed my pregnancy, I knew I was not going to have this child. I had always known I was not going to have this child, conceived in this relationship. The relationship was over. In some ways it had never begun.

From the very first moment I saw Vincent I knew there was going to be something very powerful and intense between us. We had been together before, in many lifetimes. I recognised him instantly. If you asked me how I knew, I wouldn't be able to explain. The answer doesn't lie in my head. It lies in my heart and my soul memory. I remembered him.

I knew, deep inside of me, that Vincent would be the father of my fourth child. I tried to make it different. But I knew that however hard I tried I couldn't change the truth of what I had to learn. It wouldn't work. I was meant to learn what I was meant to learn in this life. And sure enough, out of the blue, without any good reason for doing so, and at the end, the very end, of our relationship, I became pregnant.

I was shocked and I wasn't shocked. I was astonished at the timing of it but I loved the fact that we had created a child between us. The knowledge that this child would be carried for no longer than a few weeks made the experience very intense, deeply poignant. Bitter sweet. I loved carrying Vincent's child for that short time. I felt a closeness to him that I had never felt while in relationship with him. We were connected in my womb. It was a connection that I would always feel despite wanting to rid myself of it, to tear it out, rip it out, destroy it. It was a connection that shaped my life for a long while.

One of the things that I said to my child at that time was, "You have chosen to come to me, knowing that I would never give birth to you. Thank you for choosing me to be with for this short while." I knew this would be the very last time that I would be pregnant in this lifetime and I wanted to enjoy the creativity of the experience; the sense of carrying an embryo inside me; the miracle of a life developing in my womb.

It may sound strange to say this but I felt very blessed. I knew that she was a girl. I loved the feeling of fullness in my belly, the swelling of my breasts, the change in my scent. I loved the irrational hungers I had and the longings to lie down and rest. Creativity was simply happening inside me. I remembered the feeling from my other pregnancies, the intense wonder at my body and its wisdom.

I felt desolate at times, too. What was I doing? Was I mad? Here I was bonding with a child I would never see, never hold, never love. My fantasy of the very worst thing that could happen to me had always been having an abortion. Up until that point in my life I didn't know I was capable of it. And yet here I was, living my nightmare. I was planning to abort this child whom I had felt for a long time was going to come to me. Here I was, the mother of three children, planning to kill my fourth child.

I am using the word 'kill' deliberately. I know it is an emotive word and one that many will disagree with. However, I felt I needed to grasp the full reality of what I was doing. I didn't want to deny the fact that in my mind I was saying NO to a life. I knew that if I didn't intervene, the end of the process would be the birth of a child. So it seemed to me that my intervention was deliberately cutting short the potential of a life. To me, having an abortion was not an act of contraception, although I can understand that it is for many people. I just couldn't see it that way.

To me it was a much more deliberate act, much more calculated. It was more like a life choice. Did I want to have this child? Did I have the emotional resources to bring another child into the world? Was she meant to be born? The answer, very clearly, was NO. I didn't feel that she wanted life. No, I didn't have the emotional resources to bring another child into this world.

I believed she had chosen to come to me knowing I would not have a child by this man. She had known that, as I had known that. I felt I was being presented with one of the greatest challenges of my life and I wondered whether I had the strength to go through with it, to learn what I was meant to learn. It was a choice between my life and her life. In giving life to her, I would no longer be able to give life to myself. And I had just started to live again.

I remember feeling amazed when my GP seemed to refer to my termination as if it was a form of contraception that I had selected. He asked me if I would like to be sterilised at the same time as having the abortion. I was shocked at his suggestion, unable to cope with the implications of it, unable to see the termination of my child's life as a form of contraception to be made permanent by sterilisation.

I knew I was destroying a life. I knew, because I had been pregnant three times before and had connected early on to my children while they were in the womb. With my two younger children, I had known the very moment that they were conceived. From that moment, I had started to feel different in my body. I could sense the changes that were going on. I had looked at pictures of embryos at one week, two weeks, four weeks. I had known every stage of their development. I had read and studied in great detail all the books on pregnancy and labour. I'm like that. I like to know what's going on inside me, to question it and to understand it.

I understood that I was destroying this life. I felt she knew it too. My relationship with Vincent was over. It had never flowered in the way that I wanted it to. I had felt very disappointed and sad while coming to terms with this loss of love but I knew it was not a relationship into which I could contemplate bringing a child. I was being realistic, practical, down-to-earth. I was helped in this by the relationship I was developing with my child. I felt that we were in this together and going through the experience together. I also felt that I wanted to honour her choice not to be born to me.

Maybe if she had been my first pregnancy it might have been different. But she was my fourth. I had already spent several years as a single parent of three small children and I knew the incredible hard work it entailed. It had never been my conscious choice to be a one-parent family. Becoming so had made me face my preconceptions of family life and had also made me realise some of my strengths. I loved my children dearly, passionately, and loved watching them grow and develop, but alone I found the physical work very demanding.

I dreaded being woken in the night. I dreaded the feeling of exhaustion that accompanied me all the next day. I found it difficult to have my freedom restricted. I liked to be independent and adventurous. I found the structures needed to bring up children very difficult to incorporate into my life, especially after my husband left. I longed to able to do what I liked, when I liked and how I liked.

So, having finally adjusted, as best I could, to single-parent familyhood and having begun to appreciate some of its benefits, I wasn't going to go into it all over again. I was many years older and very much wiser. And I knew that I would be doing it on my own again. As far as I was concerned there was no choice. Or, closer to the truth, I didn't hesitate in the choice I made.

There were times when I cried for hours at the decision I was making; when my body felt racked with grief; when my heart ached and ached and I asked myself, "What are you doing, Isabella? Are you sure you want to do this?" The answer that came back to me was always the same: "Yes, I DO know what I am doing. Yes, I do want to do this."

The arrangements for termination of pregnancy are easy.

When my test proved positive, I immediately rang a private clinic. Within days I had an appointment. Within an hour of the appointment, I was being offered an abortion. I saw a counsellor. She was good, and I told her so. She didn't know that I too was a counsellor. She listened. She created a space for me to talk. I felt accepted by her. But I felt unreal.

Everything felt unreal. I felt very distant from the events I was living through. I was told that I would have to wait until the foetus was at least seven weeks old before they could perform the termination. Because I had known I was pregnant so early on, they offered me a pill I could take to induce a miscarriage. I could take it that very week. I declined this option. It felt too fast, as if I would be brushing the pregnancy away before connecting with it. I couldn't do that. It wasn't in my nature. I also felt it would be disrespectful to the spirit of the child who had chosen to come to me. She had her own work to do. She too had a reason for being. I didn't know what that was but it didn't feel right to rid myself of her precipitously. I knew that we needed to be together for a certain amount of time.

I arranged a time for the termination that meant I would have to carry the child for at least another two weeks. This was because of arrangements in my life that couldn't be altered, that I didn't want to alter. I didn't want to draw attention to myself by changing anything. I knew this meant I would be feeling more and more pregnant as time went on, that I would be more and more in touch with my pregnancy. And, indeed, that was what happened.

I started to feel very nauseous and bad-tempered: morning sickness overwhelmed me; morning sickness and evening sickness. It seemed to me that I felt sick all day. My breasts enlarged and became sensitive. My nipples darkened. My bras started to feel tight and constraining. My belly rounded. I felt uncomfortable wearing anything tight around my waist.

I contemplated the miracle of life in my body. Was I beginning to show, I wondered? I told a couple of friends, but only a couple. I realised that I didn't want to talk about what was happening to me. I didn't want to have to explain things. And at some level I felt ashamed of having 'got pregnant'. It seemed to be a mistake I had made that I could somehow have avoided by being more careful. At another level I was relishing this experience of pregnancy. I felt in touch with my fertility and my body. I was full of wonder at the female shape.

The two weeks passed and with the passing of time I reconciled myself to the action I was about to take. The day of the abortion came. I was almost nine weeks pregnant. I was feeling nauseous. Vincent drove me to the clinic and left me there, outside the front door. I rang the doorbell nervously. The green door opened and I was invited into the waiting room. It seemed to be full of teenage girls with their mothers. I wished that Vincent had come inside with me. But then he wasn't my partner, mother or husband. I didn't even know if he was my friend.

There were women of all ages waiting, like me, pregnant. We sat silently, looking at the floor. The teenage girls whispered. The older women, like me, were quiet. We waited until our names were called. They called a group of five or six of us at a time. How did they choose us? I went with my group to our room. There were six beds in the room. I chose a bed by the window. Silently we undressed and waited for our pre-medication. A few of the women started to tell the stories that had brought them there that day. I felt comforted, although I didn't tell mine.

I lay on the bed, dozing. I had taken Arnica for shock, and Rescue Remedy. Many years before I had studied homoeopathy. It was a time when my children were all small and seemed to get incessant and recurring infections. I decided that antibiotics were not the answer for these ills and took the children to a homoeopath. She was one of the breed of homoeopaths who like to educate their clients. I attended her courses and, over time, acquired a large range of remedies which I was able to prescribe confidently to my children instead of antibiotics with excellent results.

I lay on the bed, trying not to think about what was going to happen to me. Some time later in the morning, they called us up to the operating theatre. We went, all in a line, with our white gowns on. "You might feel a little sick when you come round," we were told. "It's the effect of the anaesthetic." I knew that already. I had had my tonsils out at the age of twenty-eight and my overriding memory is of being violently sick. They had had to give me an injection to calm the spasms that seemed to take over my body. I didn't want to be sick today.

I remember lying on the trolley outside the operating theatre feeling fogged up, while I waited for my turn. Lying there aware that there was someone in there before me and there would be someone in there after me. All these babies, all these spirits, being cut off from their mothers, returning to the spirit world. "Two minutes, that's all the time it takes," I was told. Two minutes didn't seem long enough. Long enough for what?

Was I really going to go through with this? I could hardly believe it was me lying there. I didn't feel like me at all. This wasn't the sort of event that happened in my life. I found it hard to grasp what I was doing.

"You can change your mind," the nurse told me. "You can change your mind right up until you have the general anaesthetic." I didn't change my mind and the last thing I remember was the nurse giving me an injection.

I came round in a room where there were several nurses walking around. As I opened my eyes someone leaned over me and asked if I was all right. "You have just had an abortion," she said. "The doctor will be coming round to see you later and tell you about it. Try not to drink too much, or you might feel very sick."

I was longing for a glass of water to swallow, but I lay there struggling to connect with myself. I still felt as if I was in a dream, that it was not the real me who was going through this. The real me was somewhere else and very soon I would wake up from this nightmare and be back in my familiar world with the Isabella that didn't have abortions. I still found it hard to comprehend the fact that I had just ended the life of a child, my child, our child.

I longed for Vincent. I wanted him to take me in his arms and kiss me and hold me and tell me that everything would be all right in the end. I longed for him to say, "I love you." I longed for a fairytale ending to this nightmare that I was living through. I felt as if I had strayed into a world of alien beings; a world of people I couldn't relate to. I had joined this world of people who had abortions. It was a devastating realisation. Was this really me?

The trolley took me back to my room with six beds. I lay in my bed by the window. I looked out of the window. I heard one of the other women say, "Thank goodness that's all over. I don't feel sick any more." One of the other women laughed, relieved that she had got through the experience. I lay silently, not feeling like talking or laughing. Tears rolled down my cheeks. I felt empty — empty and sad. I took another Arnica for the shock.

Sometime later the doctor came to see us all. When he came to my side, he confirmed that I had been pregnant and that the foetus had been about eight weeks old. He confirmed that I was no longer pregnant.

I had a sudden irrational desire to ask him for the blood and the aborted foetus. I didn't know if I should, though. I hadn't heard of anyone doing that. I felt silly and remained silent. To this day I wish I had had the courage to ask for the foetus. I would have buried her somewhere. I think it would have helped me to look at her, to see what I had done, to make a real connection with my experience, to connect with her. I had an overwhelming desire to touch blood, her blood, my blood. I wanted to hold the remains of my baby in my hands and experience the feel of this little human life.

Instead, I just had a blank space that I had to fill with my imagination. I imagined that there must have been a lot of blood as well as a foetus. I imagined what the foetus must have looked like, having been swished and swirled and sucked and scraped out of my body. I wondered if she felt any fear, if she had known what was happening to her. I wondered where her spirit had gone and what she would be doing now. I also wondered if I was slightly mad thinking these things. Was it healthy to think this way?

Later, in the early afternoon, we were told to get dressed

and wait in a day room until we were collected. The sun was shining into the day room. It was cold outside. My children were away visiting friends for a few days with their father. I had told their father where I was going and what I was doing. I had told him in case anything happened to me while I was under the general anaesthetic.

Vincent came. I could hardly look at him. I pretended I was all right; I had survived, I was through it. He took me home. The next day he went away and I was left on my own. I felt hollow and empty, desolate and sad. I lived through the next few days as if in a daze, not really believing what I had done, not really believing that I was capable of having an abortion.

A week later I started to cry. I cried as if my heart was breaking. I cried so much I thought I had no more tears left in my body. I wanted to cry with Vincent. I wanted to cry with him because I wanted to be able to share my grief with him. It seemed that only he would do. I did cry with Vincent, once. He comforted me as I needed to be comforted. But after that he too found it very hard.

"Do you have to make such heavy weather of all this?" he said. "You're making an awful fuss you know." His words cut into my heart. I had no words to answer him. I had no words. I stopped seeing him.

My body ached to be held and rocked and comforted. My breasts were still enlarged but I didn't feel sick any more. I was bleeding again and would do so for several days. It was strange, seeing my blood. I hadn't had a period for over two months and it was strange. I touched my blood. I watched it flow out of me, deep red, wound red. I stared at it as it dripped down my legs. I stood in the garden and let it drip onto, into, the earth. The blood dripped down my legs, the blood flowing from my womb and I thought of my child who was no longer inside me. My heart ached.

It was several weeks before my breasts returned to their normal size and my stomach to its original shape. I had put on weight during those few weeks of pregnancy. My clothes felt tight around my waist. It was a bleak time. Very little had meaning for me. The six months that followed were a nightmare. I worked tremendously hard. I lived as if in a dream, pushing out energy like pumping up a balloon, for protection, for padding.

I awoke every night at three in the morning. Fear racked my body. Fear engulfed me. "Is this how you felt as you were sucked out of my body?" I asked her. Was I being made to experience what she had experienced? "Is this my punishment?" I asked her. But there was no answer. None that I could hear, anyway.

And then it was July, that July morning. The previous six months made some sort of sense. Then the balloon burst and I cracked.

CHAPTER FIVE

"So, I *was* still pregnant after all," I said to myself. I wanted to say the words out loud. I wanted to scream them out. I wanted to yell from the rooftops: "I was pregnant after all! I was right! No wonder I still felt pregnant all those months! No wonder my body didn't return to normal after I aborted my baby! No wonder! No wonder! No wonder!" All my self-doubt, my self-criticism, my judging of my inner reality had been irrelevant.

My body *had* known its truth. I had known my truth in my heart but hadn't trusted what I knew. I had tried to bury my intuition, to suppress my inner knowledge, by getting on with my life as if the experience was all over once the abortion had taken place. But I had had some glimmer of deep, primordial feminine wisdom that had risen up from the very depths of my being, through every cell of my body. I had, after all, known my truth.

I had known I was still pregnant — not at a physical level but at a psychic level, a subtle level, an archaic level. And then I had been visited by my child in the early morning of her birth day as if she had been announcing her arrival. I hadn't known what her visitation meant and I wasn't ready to be propelled into the experience of labour and giving birth.

That is the only way that I could describe it. My body had gone into labour. I had had contractions that had increased steadily in pain and intensity as the labour progressed. I had pushed my baby out of me as only a mother who has pushed a baby into the world knows how to do. I had pushed and pushed and had known the moment she had been born. It was the moment when I lay on the bed feeling spent and drained but supremely joyful, when I had felt the presence of my spirit child in the room with me. My heart had opened with love; it was as if I had come home.

I realised that this giving birth had catapulted me into a different level of consciousness, one that I was unprepared to experience and of which I had no prior knowledge. It seemed to be out of this world. I realised it was an initiation, although into what I didn't know at that moment. I just felt a deep sense of love and being loved, of joy and happiness and of being surrounded by spirit beings full of light. I was in a state of bliss.

My pregnancy, or rather the process of pregnancy, had continued in my body even though I had denied it. I had spent six months and six days trying to live my life in a normal manner, suppressing what my inner wisdom was trying to tell me — this powerful sense that a part of me was still pregnant. At some deep, inner, subtle level, I had carried my child to term. It seemed that I hadn't killed her. She lived, she had been born. I had felt as if I had held her to my heart, had held her in my heart. This was truly an experience of transformation.

For three days and nights I lived an out-of-the-ordinary experience. I felt as if I had gone on a transformational journey. But then the magic wore off and it was time to come back. When I did, I landed with a great force which my body found acutely painful. I cracked open and lay, vulnerable and anxious, white flesh exposed, unable to communicate my experience of mystical transcendence, of beauty and light, of colour and magic, to those around me. It was an effort to speak. Words didn't seem to convey what I wanted them to communicate. I wanted others to know what I had gone through but I struggled to make myself clear. I convinced myself that those around me would describe me as having an overactive imagination; that I would be judged as oversensitive and irrational. I thought there must be something deeply amiss with my psyche because I had undergone this extraordinary, magical, mystical experience.

I realised that the experience of giving birth to my spirit child had catapulted me into another world and that that world was 'somewhere else'. It wasn't on this planet, but the 'somewhere else' that I had visited had felt deeply familiar. I had recognised the place. I had remembered it from old. It had felt like returning to a state of bliss and ecstasy. It had felt like 'going home'.

But now I was back in my ordinary, everyday world, surrounded by familiar things and familiar people. Only they were no longer familiar. It dawned on me, gradually, over the following days, that it was I who had changed. I had changed fundamentally, out of all recognition, after the powerful, transformational experience I had gone through. I had become someone else, and I was the only one who knew it. I had been opened to a level of consciousness, sensitivity and awareness that would change the way I lived the rest of my life.

I knew now that there was a world beyond the physical, material world that we see around us every day. I knew that in this world, beyond time and space, we were able to live in freedom, unhampered by the density of our bodies, by the materialism of our minds. In this world we could live in harmony, in beauty, in light and in Love. I had felt as if I were made of light, as if I were full of light: a Light Being, filled with Divine Love. I flowed with the rhythm of Life, with the rhythm of Oneness.

In that world we were able to communicate with each other in an intuitive manner. In fact our thoughts travelled as soon as they had been shaped, so we couldn't hide behind the deception of words. There was no deception at all in the world I had visited. There was no need of it.

It was a world filled with spirit beings, where we had the opportunity to be in an extraordinary relationship with Nature. Nature could speak to us and allow us to experience what it feels like to be a tree or a rock or a mountain or a cloud. It was a world where we could return to being water, air, fire or earth, where we could recall this eternal knowledge.

I gradually realised that what had happened over the three days after the birth of my spirit child was that I had begun to remember. I wasn't clear what it was I had forgotten, but I had had glimpses of memories that seemed to be returning to me, memories so beautiful, so transcendent, so mystical — unearthly Light.

Where did this memory come from? Not from this life that I am living now. So from what life? Did it mean I had remembered some past life? I had never really given much thought to the subject of past lives, although I knew that a lot has been written about their reality and their influence on the present. I was a practical person and the more esoteric levels of life frightened me. I didn't delve into them — or rather had not until this point in time. But now this sense of remembering had taken hold of me. Could it be that I had returned to a soul state, which I have read we go to between incarnations? What was a soul state? How would I recognise it? The questions remained in my mind for days.

And now that I had returned to my own familiar world, I recognised that I could see the life around me in a new way. I could really *see* all the things that surrounded me. It was as if a veil that had been drawn down over them had been lifted and all things were visible again: my children, the animals, the plants, the kitchen, the car, the television.

And I could hear again all the sounds of everyday life in a heightened manner. I could hear the telephone ringing. What a harsh sound it made! It hurt my ears. The world seemed full of noises that hurt my ears. The children's voices seemed loud and raucous, the sound of traffic was thunderous. All the sounds of life seemed to bump up sharply against me. The very air seemed to hurt my skin.

I walked about in dazed confusion, feeling I could no longer cope with the demands of everyday life. I felt as if I had been knocked on the head. I was dizzy and disoriented. And I had heartache. After the euphoria of the experience started to wear off, I became aware of this deep, deep ache in my heart, very physical and very real. It was a stabbing, hot, continuous ache and nothing would make it go away. It became a part of my life.

I took to swimming in my local swimming pool. I would lie submerged in the water, hoping it would wash away the pain; hoping that being in the water would return me to the state of feeling at one with the ocean. But it didn't. The water felt cool against my skin as I closed my eyes and let my mind wander back to my yesterdays. I lay there for hours on end, my skin becoming wrinkly and waterlogged. In the end I did find a sort of peace in the local swimming pool that summer.

And with the peace came the tears. How I cried! I cried for the place I had been to and could no longer return to: the place that had felt so much like home. I would disappear into a corner, huddle up against a wall and hold myself tightly. I would weep as if my heart was breaking. "I want to go home," I would whisper to myself, not even knowing where home was or indeed how to get there. "I want to go home," I moaned to myself like an animal in pain. And, like an animal, I wanted to slink away and be on my own until I felt better. I didn't want to be with people, with my children or with my friends. I just wanted to be with myself, where I didn't have to explain anything to anyone.

I didn't know who I was any more. I could no longer be the person I had been. The experiences I had been through had changed all that. I looked ahead to the future and felt frightened of it. I looked back at the past and longed to return there. It seemed safe and secure. I had known who I was then — a mother, a single parent of three teenage children. A counsellor and a trainer of counsellors. A supervisor and, occasionally, a consultant. I had a clear idea of what I believed in and who my friends were. Life seemed simple as I looked back.

But the past was over and everything had changed. Others around me went on with their lives and on the outside I did too. On the inside I felt fragmented, vulnerable, frightened and insecure. On the outside I was surrounded by children, friends, acquaintances. On the inside I was totally alone.

I felt as if there was no one I could talk to about the experiences I had been through. I'm sure that there *were* people I could have talked to, but I was ashamed, embarrassed and terrified that I might be classified as insane. "No, talking to people is too dangerous, Isabella," I said to myself. I was ashamed to think that my words wouldn't make sense to them.

I was embarrassed that I couldn't intellectualise my experience. A part of me felt that I had 'got it all out of proportion', that I was being 'irrational, illogical'. Little did I realise how important that breakthrough would be in my work and in my life. For someone who had lived her life in an intellectual, thinking manner, to be left without words was probably one of the scariest things that could happen. It was as if I had no defences to hide behind, no way to make sense to myself and others. My experience had been wordless, so any words that I chose to describe it would limit it, contain it, give it a form. How could I give it a form when it had been an experience of formlessness, of boundary transcendence, of the Divine?

I lived through the remainder of that summer as if in a haze, a hazy daze. The days came and went. Breakfast, lunch, tea and dinner, bed; breakfast, lunch, tea and dinner, bed; again and again, day after day. The sun rose, the sun set. Sometimes I saw it and sometimes I didn't. The butterflies danced on the buddleia as they had done earlier in the season. This time I hardly noticed them. At night, I looked up at the stars outside my bedroom window but they just seemed very far away. I tried to look for the star that I had released into the night sky but it wasn't there or I couldn't see it. My eyes didn't want to look.

I sat under the silver birches in my garden and tried to listen to their language but all I could hear was the cry in my own heart. The silver birches belonged to a different world, into which I no longer had an entry. I sat in my garden and wept. I wept for the language of the trees that I could no longer understand, for the connection with the earth that I no longer felt. I wept for the golden shimmery glow that had surrounded me for three days and the iridescent colours I had seen everywhere. I wept for the sound that had resonated in my heart that had carried a vibration identical to my own. And I wondered whether I had imagined everything after all. Had I imagined the world that had opened up to me and that no longer seemed accessible?

The world was drab and desolate, devoid of gentleness and softness, understanding and love, colour and ease. It seemed to be a place of grey and concrete. It hurt to talk. My throat felt tight and my words came out tactlessly and clumsily. What had happened to my intuitive communication, the language that had seemed to flow from my heart? I did try to talk but I felt foolish and tongue-tied, like a small child trying to catch a grown-up's attention and, having got it, not being able to say anything.

I closed my practice for six weeks. I knew I was unfit for work. I had no more teaching commitments until very late in the summer. The children were on holiday and their presence and activities were all I could cope with. Their love and unconditional acceptance touched me deeply. "I wonder what they would think of me if I told them?" I asked myself. "What would they say if they knew that they might have had a baby sister now?" I pictured myself as the mother of four children. "I couldn't have done it," I said to myself. "I just couldn't have done it."

I lay in the sun when it shone but the heat of it inflamed the pain in my heart. I stopped lying in the sun and instead sat in the cool shade of the silver birches; my little grove of silver birches that had given me such enchanted moments not long before. I knew that they were still enchanted trees although I no longer shared their language. I would sit with my back against the trunk of the oldest tree and feel its bark through my thin cotton shirt. If I looked carefully enough, I could see all kinds of wildlife scurrying around inside the cracks in the bark. One day there were ladybirds of all shapes and sizes sitting in the cracks. I counted the spots on their backs. I went back day after day and gazed at the ladybirds, counting the spots on their backs. I became totally absorbed by their activities.

In the bushes I found a spider. I watched her endlessly. She was small and neat; busy and dedicated to her job of weaving the threads, creating the world into which some other minute creature would fall. I picked up a pencil and paper and started to write without really knowing what I was doing or why.

There is a spider in my garden,
It is making a web. No!
It is not an 'it', it is a 'she'
She is making 'her' web, not 'a' web.
There is a spider in my garden
she is making her web
No, she is not 'making' her web
she is 'weaving' her web.

There is a spider in my garden
she is weaving her web
she is weaving her web for all to see.
She has chosen a place where the rosebushes grow.

Her web is poised between the pruned branches of the
summer rose at the bottom of my garden. It is a shady place,
a safe place.

I watch the spider weave her web.
She is beautiful.
She is creating her world.
She is creating her world as I create mine.
I am the spider and
I create my world, spun with silver threads.

My beautiful world.

I don't know where the words came from but I know that in writing them down I felt peaceful again, peaceful and momentarily content. While writing I had forgotten my heartache, forgotten my surroundings. I had enjoyed the writing and becoming immersed in the world of the spider. It had been the same when I looked at the ladybirds. I became connected to my inner world but in a contented, peaceful way, not in a suffering way. I had had too much suffering over the last few months. I read the poem over and over again, enjoying the words, relishing them, feeling renewed and refreshed.

I'm not a fool. I knew I needed help of some kind. I was

isolating myself more and more. Inside myself I was descending into a pit of loneliness, guilt, sorrow and, most frightening of all, a well of nothingness. I was beginning to doubt what had happened to me. I was beginning to doubt my reality. The silver thread that kept me connected to the unseen world was my memory of the baby that I had seen in my mind's eye that summer morning.

If I closed my eyes, I could see her still quite clearly. She never changed her position. She always wore the same little dress with ducks embroidered on it. She still wore the white cotton bonnet. She still slept. My child, my spirit child. I imagined what it would be like if she was here with me now. If I had a baby, a real newborn baby, one that I could hold and love. "I would be breastfeeding her now," I thought to myself. I looked back to those early days of mothering my three children and recalled how immersed I had become in all the paraphernalia of their first few weeks of life. They were so demanding and all-consuming; they were so dependent. They were so utterly lovable, so easy to love.

Only this time there was no newborn baby. There had been a birth, yes, and a labour, and I had felt her presence in the room with me, but I could not hold her to me and feel her little body against mine. I couldn't smell her: that wonderful smell that babies have: all milky and sweet. I couldn't touch her soft baby skin. She had no solid form; she didn't belong to this physical world. I couldn't show her to my friends and family. She was a secret child, a spirit child, known only to me, and known only to me in spirit.

I pictured her asleep in her pram at the bottom of the garden, under the silver birches. The pram would be covered by netting to protect her from midges and cats. I imagined what my life would be like now if she were here with me: if she were a reality in my life. "How different this summer would have been if I had gone ahead and had her," I thought. A summer baby, born when the moon was full. My fourth child, my unseen child, my secret child.

My heart yearned for her. I couldn't look at other babies in prams; it was too painful. I kept wondering what it would have been like if I had been pushing the pram or rocking her or breastfeeding her. "NO! I must stop thinking this way!" I chided myself, self-critical as always. "I could really go mad if I go on like this. I'm being morbid." But the truth was that I was very depressed and whatever I tried to do, whatever I tried to involve myself in, didn't take my mind off the presence of my spirit child. She was all around me. She was inside me. She was in my heart. And my heart was breaking.

One afternoon, late in the summer, I sat at the bottom of the garden with my ex-husband, the father of my three children, and I wept. I was inconsolable in my grief. "I think I'm having a breakdown, Geoffrey," I cried out to him. "I feel as if I'm going mad. Everything is crumbling around me. I feel as if I have nothing to hold on to and I'm so scared. What shall I do? Please help me!"

He was silent for a while and then said, "Have you thought of going back into therapy?"

I had already spent seven years in therapy and the idea didn't feel right to me at all. Going into therapy would be like going backwards. I didn't want to go backwards. I wanted to go forwards. I wanted to move forward, through and out of this experience. In my heart I knew that what I had been through had opened me up to influences and energies which I could no longer explore by delving into the past. I knew it was time for something different. A different kind of therapy, a different kind of healing; a very different journey altogether.

For a start, I still felt unable to talk. Words were still stumbling blocks to me. Other people were as if on the other side of glass. I moved my mouth and they moved their mouths, but the words didn't connect with my experience. It was as if I couldn't hear them and they couldn't hear me. I was very aware that I needed help but going back into therapy was not it. So, once again, I discarded the suggestion.

He tried again: "Why don't you go to see your GP?" This frightened me. With my family's history of mental instability, I feared that I might be referred to a psychiatrist and I didn't want to be given any antidepressants, sleeping pills or tranquil-lisers. However painful the experience I was going through, I knew I wanted to stay fully present throughout it.

Anyway, I didn't want to put my health and healing into the hands of the medical profession. Maybe I was being stubborn but I didn't believe that they had the resources available to help me through this crisis. This was not a crisis of my physical body. This was an emotional and spiritual crisis. And the help I needed was in those areas.

It was at this moment, this darkest of moments, when I had finally admitted to another human being how I was feeling, when I had finally called out for help, that I recalled a conversation with a colleague of mine. She had stayed at a place in Dorset: a healing centre. "Each room is painted a different colour," she had told me. I particularly remembered that piece of information. I found it reassuring. I liked the reasoning behind it. Researchers throughout the centuries have acknowledged the profound influence of colour on our physical, mental, emotional and spiritual well-being and colour therapy is an ancient healing art. I called her that evening.

"Yes, I know the place you want," she said. "I think it will be perfect for you. It's called Middle Piccadilly."

It sounded the right place for me. I had never been anywhere like it before. In fact the word 'healing' would have put me off in the past, so rigid was my thinking. I telephoned the very next morning and made a reservation with them for three days. I was to stay in the room they called 'Cranberry'. My healing journey had begun.

Chapter Six

Middle Piccadilly! Even the name has a magical ring to it I thought to myself as I drove down on that late summer afternoon. It was a beautiful day, hot and sunny, and the countryside looked wonderful. I could see it all around me but I felt so heavy in my heart that I couldn't appreciate its beauty. I was longing to get there and the drive seemed to be taking for ever.

Finally I arrived. I drove up to the 17th-century thatched farmhouse wondering what was going to happen to me when I got inside. I felt very nervous and a little desperate. Nervous because I had never done anything quite like this before and desperate because I felt that if I couldn't find what I needed here then I wouldn't know where to turn next.

I had read, very carefully, all the information I had been sent when I confirmed my booking at Middle Piccadilly Natural Healing Centre. "We provide a caring atmosphere where, through a wide range of holistic therapies, we promote the process of self-healing," the brochure said. I believed in their philosophy. I knew I was the only one who could heal myself. And I knew that I needed help and support with that process.

The brochure went on to say:

Natural healing deals with all forms of disease through treatment of the whole being — mind, emotions, body and spirit — rather than concentrating on specific symptoms and ailments. We do not believe in quick remedies, which may relieve symptoms, temporarily helping the process of healing, but which, in fact, may hinder the natural attempts of the body to bring itself into balance.

I had learnt, through my own therapeutic journey and through working with clients, that the process of change is a gradual one. In the end there are no quick solutions or short cuts.

In our therapies our aim is to help this natural healing process to take place and, recognising that each individual is unique, we investigate and advise on the complete life pattern of the patient. This initial consultation lasts one hour and the therapist will recommend the most appropriate treatment plan. We ask you to arrive between 4 and 5 pm so that you can be given a diagnostic session before the evening meal. At this session a series of coordinated treatments will be programmed especially for you.

Well, here I was, arriving on time at 5 pm. I wondered what would happen next. I didn't have long to wait. A kind-looking elderly man welcomed me warmly and took my bag to my room, the one called 'Cranberry'. Cranberry was a mixture of magenta and red with a touch of purple in the decorations! The man introduced himself as Gerry Harvey.

"Middle Piccadilly is a small family-run concern," he said, "and you will see Eliana Harvey for your initial diagnostic consultation. But you have time to make yourself a cup of tea first, if you would like one." He then left me with a detailed information sheet to fill in.

A little while later I met Eliana for my consultation. She introduced herself and told me that she and her husband Gerry were the co-founders of Middle Piccadilly. "We were very attracted to Middle Piccadilly by its atmosphere of absolute peace," she explained, "and our guests obviously find this so as well. Some of them return time and again to restore and renew themselves with the various complementary therapies we offer. But this is your first visit, so tell me a little of what has brought you here."

I found myself blurting everything out to her. I told her

about the abortion and how I still felt overwhelmed with grief about it, although I had known that it was absolutely right for me to have it. I told her a little about my past history. The tears flowed down my cheeks as I sat in the peaceful room and told a complete stranger shreds of my life story. I can't remember if she said anything to me other than that I needed to modify my usual breakfast as she felt it was too heavy for my liver! Part of the information sheet I had filled in prior to the consultation had asked me for full details of all my meals.

After the consultation I was given a treatment plan. It looked interesting. The consultation was followed by an early supper. "Delicious vegetarian wholefood cuisine with our own organic produce whenever possible," the brochure had said. It *was* delicious. And very nourishing to have a meal put in front of me that I hadn't had to think about or shop for. I felt very strange being away from home. I couldn't remember the last time I had been away on my own like this, without the children. I went to bed early and slept like a log!

The next morning I had my first session with a therapist. It was a reflexology treatment followed by an aromatherapy massage. My therapist was called Colette. I saw her card: Colette Prideaux-Brune I.F.A., M.I.I.R., I.T.E.C. it read. Colette is a highly respected aromatherapist/reflexologist with fourteen years' experience in her work. I found the reflexology session blissful. I asked Colette to tell me how reflexology worked.

"Reflexology is a science based on the principle that there are reflexes in the feet relative to each and every organ and all parts of the body," she said. "It is a technique that has been used for many thousands of years by the Chinese and the Egyptians. I can assess a patient's health and treat disorders by working the whole of both feet and stimulating the body's natural healing process. This is a totally different approach from that of using drugs which in themselves suppress the body's natural healing efforts. It's known that at least 75 per cent of disease is caused by stress. Reflexology strengthens the nerves and blood supply and helps to restore and maintain equilibrium."

"How do you assess a person's health?" I asked her.

"I feel for a person's energy levels and then I go to specific areas and check for energy, toxins or blockages. I fill in a record sheet as I go along. Here's your record sheet." She held up a piece of paper that had two feet drawn on it. Some areas were shaded in and others had notes written beside them. "Now I'm going to tune in to your body intuitively to assess which level I need to work on in the aromatherapy session — the physical, emotional, mental, spiritual or past life level."

I asked her to tell me about aromatherapy. She explained that the use of aromatic oils on the body goes back 2000 years before Christ when records show that plants and their essential oils were being used for medical and religious purposes. "Every living thing has a life force, energy or 'soul'," she said. "It is believed that the life force of a plant is contained in its essential oil and through aromatherapy we introduce this life force into the body. I'm going to give you a full body massage lasting about one and a half hours which will stimulate your lymph flow and blood circulation, which in turn will speed up the elimination of toxic waste in the body."

"How are you going to choose the oils?" I asked her.

"I'm going to let the oils speak to me through dowsing. The reflexology has indicated that the energy in your womb is very blocked, that there is a lot of grief held in your heart and lungs and that your energy levels are low, especially in the kidneys. The kidneys hold fear."

Tears welled up into my eyes as I listened to her and I felt a lump in my throat. My body was speaking for itself and I had found a way to communicate, without words, what had been going on for me over the past few months. Colette knew. She had tuned in to my body and it had spoken to her. It was like a miracle! I felt understood at a very deep level, well beyond words.

"What oils have you chosen?" I asked as I noticed that she had set aside three bottles.

"Jasmine to help release the blocked energy and trauma in the womb, Sandalwood to nourish and give warmth to that kidney energy and Lavender to help heal your grief and help you to relax generally."

Then I surrendered to the glorious experience of a full body massage with the scent of the heavenly oils. Colette put some of the warm, scented oil under my nose so that I could breathe in the wonderful aroma while she worked on my body. Towards the end of the session I felt her placing some pebbles on my body which she left there while she wrote up her notes.

When she removed the pebbles she told me that she was going to bury them in the earth in order to cleanse them of any negative energy they had absorbed from my body. I asked her if I could have her notes. She agreed and I took them away with me to read. She had written:

I used crystals in this treatment on the heart, solar plexus and base chakras. The crystals I used were smoky quartz and pebbles that absorb negative energy. I also used a crystal wand to seal Isabella's chakras as they were too open. Isabella was very spaced out and very vulnerable following the shock and trauma of the abortion and the birth and I worked hard to ground her back into her body.

Isabella had been feeling a lot of heat in her heart chakra and, as I worked on this area, I was very aware of a past life sacrifice of her heart in South America. Her heart felt like it was trapped in a cage and locked away. She used phrases like 'I feel distant', 'I feel cut off from others' and 'I feel outside the world'. The overall smell of the oils mixed together was a metallic one which relates to the lung/colon meridians. These are connected with grief.

I fell asleep shortly after reading this account of the session and didn't awake until the next meal time! I slept most of that day, only getting up for delicious meals. After supper, I had a rich mud bath which Eliana had recommended to help clear the toxins from my body. I went to bed again and slept until morning. Even then I found it almost impossible to get up. My body felt leaden, like a dead weight. I was exhausted.

My next treatment was called acupressure and I was to have it with Eliana. She told me a little about it.

"It's a painless technique using gentle fingertip pressure to balance and harmonise the body, mind and spirit through the channels known as the meridians. This system is based on ancient teachings of Chinese medicine. Acupressure can benefit many conditions, particularly backache and stress. It has a releasing effect on the emotional body, dissolving blocks and tensions. Shen Tao Acupressure is a whole-body therapy: both hands are used and treatments last an hour, giving deep relaxation."

I thought the description was pretty accurate as I came away after the hour feeling exhausted again! Eliana confirmed what Colette had diagnosed and suggested that I go and lie down until lunch time as it was very beneficial to rest after the treatments in order to derive the most benefit from them. I needed no second bidding as I took to my bed again and slept. I couldn't believe how much I was sleeping or how tired I felt. The therapists all reassured me that it was part of the healing process and very common in their guests.

"Middle Piccadilly is intended as an oasis of calm and tranquillity," they told me. "Our aim is to relieve our guests of all the pressures of modern life and for this reason we have no TV, radio or newspapers, nor is the telephone available for incoming calls except for genuine emergencies. In this way you will derive maximum benefit from your stay."

My last treatment was a Bach Flower consultation with Clare Harvey. Clare is a well-known flower essence consultant who uses a vast repertoire of essences from all corners of the world, many of which have been part of the system of medicine employed by indigenous cultures for thousands of years.

Prior to the consultation I read the information about flower remedies and gem essences:

These remedies prepared from the flowers, wild plants, bushes and trees from all over the world do not work on the physical only but also on the states of mind, mood and emotions. Worry or fear will deplete vitality and the way is laid open to sickness and disease. The remedies restore harmony and unity to mind and body, allowing the vital energies to flow freely and so promoting the body's own natural healing.

Clare's consulting room was crowded with what looked to me like hundreds of little bottles. There were bottles standing on their own, bottles in boxes, brown boxes, brightly painted boxes, boxes and bottles of different shapes and sizes — shelves and shelves of them. Clare introduced herself and told me a little of how she worked. "I use a pendulum as a diagnostic tool because it helps me to be more accurate in the selection of the remedies," she said. "I have found that straight discussion with the patient combined with a good working knowledge of the remedies does not always provide a clear enough picture of the more deep-seated problems involved." She swung a quartz crystal on the end of a silver chain. "The pendulum prevents my opinions and ideas from impinging on the selection of the essences, making the whole procedure far more objective."

She then asked me to place one finger on each bottle in turn. She gently laid her hand over mine. "This is to create a link between you and me," she explained. She held the pendulum in the other hand and I saw that it began to move as I placed my finger on the top of each bottle. Every now and again it moved in a different direction and she would pick this bottle out and set it to one side. At the end, ten bottles stood there. "These are the essences you have chosen for yourself," she said. "I acted as a mirror for you. Now I'll look to see which remedies are for the past, which for the present and which for the future." She lined them up in a certain order. "There are two essences for the past," she said. "These are to do with childhood and other early traumas and the rest are for the present situation you are in. I believe that the whole reason for prescribing flower essences is to help you become aware of your own stress patterns, enabling you to take back responsibility for your own health and happiness. So I believe it's important to inform and involve you in the whole process. I'll give you a description of what each essence is for and you can fill me in on how it relates to your life circumstance."

She then talked briefly about the body's energy systems: the aura, the chakras and the subtle bodies and how the remedies I had chosen would act on these. She explained that the aura is an electromagnetic shield that surrounds the body. All life forms possess one. The aura is different from the other energy fields known as the subtle bodies in that it is a general field of energy emanating from the physical body, whereas the subtle bodies are fixed bands of energy at set distances from the body. The seven subtle bodies are rather like the rings of Saturn surrounding the physical body. These specific layers of energy emanate from the physical body via the chakras. There are seven chakras, like portholes, located just to the front of the body along the spinal column. Chakra is the Sanskrit word meaning a wheel or a circle. The chakras are the very core of the aura. The aura, the chakras and the subtle bodies make up the major part of the subtle anatomy. Flower and gem essences affect the subtle anatomy and then filter down into the physical body.

"Now let's see which essences you have chosen," she said. "For the past you have chosen *Star of Bethlehem*, a Bach remedy for deep shock held within the body due to the struggle of being born, and *Aspen*, another Bach remedy, for apprehension and fear, a direct response to the shock. It is a fear and apprehension of not feeling safe or being safe in the world due to a lack of nourishing support in very early childhood.

"For the present situation you have chosen *Arnica*, a Flower Essence Society remedy. This is helpful for the recent shock of the abortion, the trauma to the being, and to help prevent it becoming deeply locked in the body, where it would block the body's self-healing processes. It's also for accidents or violent experiences where the soul or Higher Self dissociates from the physical body. *Chamomile* is another Flower Essence Society remedy. This is for emotional stress, upset and tension that lodges in the nervous system, which can lead to insomnia. *Indian Pink*, also a Flower Essence Society remedy, is good when you are being pressured by too many demands, mental stress, tension and worry, or when you feel depleted. It helps you to become focused and centred.

"*Ohai Ali'i* is a Hawaiian Flower Essence that helps to dissolve long-term thought patterns and structures, and mental blocks that have accumulated over past lifetimes. Such blocks can manifest in the skeletal structure. *Ettringite* is a Pegasus Essence which will help you to regain and empower yourself, bringing you a greater sense of the combination of love, power, strength, will, purpose and spiritual guidance. *Stress/Tension* is a Himalayan Aditi Essence, Aditi being the Sanskrit word for 'earth'. This flower essence is for relieving day-to-day tension and nervous stress. It relaxes tensed muscles by calming and strengthening the nervous system. It is helpful for the strains experienced by those living a fast city life and it combats all psychological and physical stresses.

"*Leafless Orchid* is an Australian Living Essence for feeling bogged down. It's for the inspired therapist who is drained, tired and lacking in energy and it gives awareness of one's own or others' central needs rather than the peripheral needs. It will help you to find the energy deep within yourself to keep positive and active in your therapeutic work without becoming depleted and tired, either mentally or physically. *Russian Kolokoltchik*, another Australian Living Essence, is a survival essence to help conquer adversity after a long period of struggle where the will to fight can sometimes fade. It restores the will to keep on fighting and not to succumb.

"Take three drops orally every morning and evening for the next four months," Clare told me. "Would you like me to give you my notes after I have written them up?"

"Yes," I replied, having found it very helpful to read Colette's following the aromatherapy session. When I read the notes later, I found they were an interesting account of how she believed the essences I had chosen related to my past and present situation.

Isabella gave one the impression of not being at home or comfortable in her body, or on the planet, due to the long, slow shock of being born into her particular family situation. Isabella did not receive the love and nurturing necessary to ground her or anchor her into her body. Fear and apprehension tend to follow from this.

I felt so tired after my consultation with Clare that I returned to my room and fell asleep again. I was meant to be driving back home that afternoon but thought it would be difficult to keep awake at the wheel, so I asked if I could stay another night. I telephoned home and was reassured to find that everyone was well and that there would be no problem if I returned the following morning.

I felt very tired for the days following my visit to Middle Piccadilly. I slept long hours and was grateful that I had closed my practice. The children were enjoying the last few days of their summer holidays and most of the time left me to rest in whatever way felt best. I was deeply grateful to them for their acceptance of my lethargic state.

I resolved to speak to my osteopath whom I had seen regularly every four weeks from the time of the abortion to the birth of my spirit child. I had been a patient of hers for many years as I believed in keeping my body well serviced for my work! I trusted her implicitly and felt it was important for me to find out as much as I could about the abortion and the subsequent experiences I had been through.

My osteopath, who wishes to remain anonymous, has been practising for sixteen years. She trained at the European School of Osteopathy, is a member of the General Council and Register of Osteopaths and will soon be a member of the General Osteopathic Council.

I started by saying, "I feel that osteopathy really helped me in my physical and emotional recovery after the abortion. Can you tell me something about how it works and why it should have been so beneficial to me?"

She explained that osteopathic treatment helps deal with both direct physical shock and emotional shock manifested in the body. "Osteopathy works very gently with the body, allowing it to recover and heal from trauma and shock," she said.

"What happened to my body during the abortion and the following six months?" I asked. Together we looked up the notes and she explained her diagnosis and treatment plan. First of all she told me that all osteopaths work within the same principles, although each osteopath might have a slightly different approach within those parameters. She said, "Osteopaths keep two major principles in mind. The first is that working with the body's structure (anatomy) can influence its functioning (physiology) and the second is that the body is a self-regulating, self-correcting, self-healing mechanism. The osteopath acts as a catalyst for those innate mechanisms that restore the body to balance. To quote Dr Still, the founder of osteopathy, 'Osteopathy gives the body back to itself.' "

That made sense to me. I did feel that her gentle and yet profound treatments had ensured my physical good health and had contributed to the recovery of my sleep. I remembered that I had begun to feel physically very well prior to the birth experience which had then plunged me into an emotional and a spiritual crisis.

"What did you find in my body after the abortion?" I asked her.

"After the abortion I made a careful assessment of your physical condition and I found several things," she said. "First, through observing the alteration in your respiratory motion (you were breathing very shallowly), I found that there was a profound shock remaining in your system which manifested principally in the poor movement of your diaphragm and upper ribs. The shock had also upset your sympathetic nervous system, as all shocks do, activating it and creating a constant state of anxiety accounting for your lack of sleep during this period.

"Secondly," she continued, "I found that there was a drag on the deep fasciae of your body resulting from the mechanical process of the pregnancy termination. This drag, although apparently local, had had effects through your whole body through the 'core' — or deep centre — connections."

"What is 'fasciae'?" I asked.

"The fasciae wrap and protect every organ in the body. Those surrounding the uterus or womb connect indirectly to those of the spine and so upwards through the 'core' of the body to the base of the cranium. I believe that through these fascial connections a drag on the cranial base can produce a drag on the pituitary, which as you know is an endocrine organ that secretes numerous hormones including those that influence the ovaries. Upset to the pituitary may impair return to normal hormonal balance; a recovery which is always difficult after the abrupt termination of hormonal production that occurs with a terminated pregnancy or a miscarriage.

"I'm among those," she added, "who consider that this drag may be partially responsible for post-natal depression after a traumatic birth where the fasciae have undergone an irreversible disturbance.

"And thirdly, I found that your pelvis was upset by the biomechanical disturbance of the abortion."

"How did you find that out?"

"Well, the relationship of the innominate bones — the haunch bone and the hip bone — to the sacrum and the lumbar spine was altered." She saw the look on my face and said, "I know. It's a lot to take in!"

By this time I was feeling very ignorant about the functioning and structure of my body and was beginning to think I should do a course in anatomy and physiology.

"This biomechanical disruption," she continued, "had then upset the nerve and vascular supplies to all the organs of the pelvis (uterus, bladder, small and large intestine). Remember what I told you at the beginning about the principles of osteopathy? Structure influences function in a reciprocal relationship."

I had privately decided that when I returned home I would look up all the information she had given me in my daughter's A-level biology book in order to shed some light on what she had described.

"Now let's look at the treatment I gave you," she said. "Are you ready?" I nodded. I was fascinated.

"First I approached your respiration through working with the motion of your diaphragm to restore a normal breathing pattern. Respiration is fundamental to life, you know!"

"I know," I said laughing. "We were always being told that in my counselling and psychotherapy training. 'BREATHE!' the trainer would say, time and time again. 'Support yourself through your breathing!' Why did you start with my breathing?"

"Because you were breathing very shallowly and that creates poor oxygenation throughout the whole system so the body cannot achieve homoeostasis. Do you know what I mean by 'homoeostasis'?"

"Not really," I said, rather gingerly.

"'Homoeo' means 'same' and 'stasis' means 'state'. Therefore homoeostasis is the chemical balance within the cells. Your shallow breathing was also upsetting the sympathetic nervous system and was impeding fascial continuity. I was working to restore your breathing to normal which not only assists homoeostasis at a cellular level, it also calms the whole nervous system and assists in lifting the fascial drag in the pelvis."

I was now beginning to feel really lost and confused by all the technical terms but I persevered.

"Secondly, I moved to the sacrum in its relationship through the sacroiliac joints to the whole pelvis, to balance the biomechanical disturbance and the associated vascular and neurological disturbances. I worked directly on your uterus making a contact above the abdomen and below the sacrum to settle its fascial relationships. I then returned to the diaphragm to integrate its movement with the balance achieved in the pelvis. The disturbance to your respiration had also affected the upper ribs, so I then worked to release them. While in this area, I set about lifting the fascial drag on the pericardium — the fascial wrapping of the heart — which had also been affected."

I was finally beginning to get a sense of the extraordinary and beautiful balance within my body. A body I had taken absolutely for granted all my life. I began to glimpse how each organ and its workings affected the others. I was shocked at how I had taken the decision to have an abortion without even thinking of the impact and profound shock to my body.

My osteopath was continuing, "I then moved to your upper cervical region (upper neck) which had been disturbed both by the fascial drag and by its internal compensation for the changes in your pelvis. I worked gently to release the tension in that area. Finally I moved to your cranium to release the tensions there and so to free the pituitary in its house of the sella turcica, a little groove in the sphenoid bone at the base of the brain.

"Over the next few months I worked with you regularly every four weeks to release your body gently out of the pregnancy, out of your loss and out of the shock to your system. The gentle approach of osteopathic treatment allowed you and your body, over time, to integrate the changes created by the treatment and to heal."

She told me that at each session she had returned to all the areas that had been disturbed to establish the effects of the treatment and to ensure that the body felt whole, integrated and settled within itself. "I worked to bring a sense of axial coordination and thus integration to the body. I hope that has all been of some help to you, Isabella."

I thanked her and came away from our meeting full of information and insight. I had found it extremely useful to go over the diagnosis and treatment plan with her and to understand more clearly how osteopathy worked. I had known intuitively that I needed to be working with my osteopath throughout that time but now my intuitive sense was anchored in very concrete terms. I felt as if I was going through a process of observing and understanding myself. I knew that it was only one way of rationalising and understanding my experience but I had always found it very helpful to grasp things at a practical level whenever I felt lost and disoriented.

The consultation with my osteopath, following on from my visit to Middle Piccadilly, brought home to me, in a very down-to-earth way, the profound shock that the abortion and the birth experience had had on my body and on my mental, emotional and spiritual state. Although I now had a greater understanding of the experiences I had been through, I still found it difficult to convey in words what I was feeling. My emotional world was still locked up, my heart still hot and heavy. I would spend hours crying by myself, the tears flowing only in private. My grief was hard to bear. At times I felt as if I was going mad with grief — for my child, for the place I had been to when she had been born, for the relationship with her father which had ended shortly before the abortion, and for myself and the situation I now found myself in. Where could I go to get away from this dark, dark place, I wondered. Autumn and winter were approaching. I had always hated the long, dark, cold nights and this year I knew they would seem even worse. I felt as if I was on the edge of a precipice and might at any moment fall off.

CHAPTER SEVEN

That autumn I had a long-standing appointment to see the psychic Betty Balcombe. I had been introduced to Betty several years before and found her wise and full of easy-to-understand knowledge and information. I would consult her every six months or so. The appointments were always made at the previous session so I never knew what would be happening in my life when the next session came round.

To Betty, being a psychic means that she is able to give healing energy to people who have an energy imbalance and are unwell, in order that they may help themselves. She can also tune in to the aura field that surrounds each of us and interpret the impressions she receives. She believes that "all reasoning beings have the right to knowledge, that no one has the perfect way of life for all and that we need to question and search our inner senses, physical knowledge, spiritual connection and soul wisdom to find our own path in life." In 1988 Betty wrote her first book *As I See It...* Her second book, *The Energy Connection*, was published in 1993.

The first time I visited Betty I very anxious. Someone had suggested that I might be a psychic and I didn't know what that meant. I was told to go and see Betty to get more information! I followed that suggestion and from it came many years of learning.

I kept full written notes of the first sessions we had. The tape recorder never seemed to pick up her voice. This, she told me, happened to her a lot. At our very first session she told me within minutes that I needed to write. She told me that counselling and psychotherapy would be all right up to a point but that I needed to write about my own experiences and my own life troubles.

"Write for the sheer joy of it!" she said. "Write from your heart!"

But, that autumn, writing was far from my mind. I was still deeply troubled about the experiences I had gone through. Although at Middle Piccadilly all the therapists had supported my own sense of being out of my body after the phantom labour, I still felt I needed to know more about what had happened and I was sure that Betty would be able to tell me. I was glad that this appointment, made so very many months ago, had come around now.

Betty immediately sensed that my energy was very low. She said, "You are very near the edge of the cliff, Isabella. What are you going to do about it?"

I told her how I was feeling, how bleak and desolate and utterly confused I was. "I don't know who I am any longer, Betty. Extraordinary things have happened to me and my heart is aching. It's an ache that can't be soothed by anything or anyone. I'm the closest I have ever felt to being broken-hearted. My life seems meaningless and futile. I don't know where I belong any more."

I sat in front of Betty and the words I had held in for so long poured out of me like a torrent. I felt as if the Ice Age inside my heart was finally coming to an end. I was finding the words to describe my experience. Words that had eluded me until now came cascading out of my mouth as I continued: "Every evening I go down to the river at sunset time and watch the Canada geese flying in low over the water to settle down for the night on the Eyot. Watching these geese affects me deeply. Tears just pour down my face. I sit on the river bank with the setting sun on my face and my heart feels like it's breaking. I feel as if I'm being called to another place, as if a part of me is somewhere else, calling to me over the water from behind the setting sun. I can hear the call so clearly in my heart. I can't make sense of it. I go down to the river because it's the only place to go. There, with the geese flying over the water, with the setting sun shining on my face, I feel I am responding to this call in my heart in the only way I know how."

As I talked, she had been writing some words down on a piece of paper. She had also started to doodle. I looked over to see what she had written. There were the main words I had used over and over again: OPEN, SUN, WATER, FLY, HOME.

"Have you thought of flying home for a holiday?" she suggested, ever practical and down-to-earth. She knew that I came from South America, a place I would have to FLY to, over WATER, and where the SUN shone all the time. She knew that this was my birthplace and so probably my HOME. She knew that there were great OPEN expanses of land.

"I don't know where home is any more," I said. I was weeping inconsolably now, rocking from side to side. "I want to go home and I don't know where it is any more."

She waited until my tears had cried themselves out and I was calmer. I sat still, shivering slightly. My nose and ears were stopped up from all the crying I had done. I was surrounded by a mass of wet tissues. But I felt calmer. I had got it all out. I had found my words. I had put words to my experience.

She then asked me what had been happening to me recently. I told her about my abortion and about the experiences I had had at the time of my child's birth. I told her that I had spent three days in another place, a place of bliss. "Everything was Light and Love and full of Beauty," I explained. "I heard the trees talk and I was in this extraordinary relationship with nature." I described how I had then returned to my physical body and had felt devastated ever since. I felt as if I couldn't cope with being me, in my body, trying to move about and relate to people. "What happened to me, Betty?" I asked. "Do you know? Can you tell me?"

She listened quietly and then told me she felt that the shock of the labour had triggered memories of my soul existence, and my feelings of being lost and homesick probably related to that state. She said it was understandable to feel confused after an experience like that. Our soul is so beautiful, ethereal and loving that it would be a profound shock to return to the physical body after connecting with it. Normally when we incarnate into a physical body we lose all memory of our true life and existence. Reconnecting with the memory causes us to 'return home to our soul' while still on Earth. When we come back to the physical plane, we bring the memories with us and these may create in us an overwhelming state of home-sickness.

"Our soul is our true self," she said. "When we live on this Earth as a physical being with spirit energy from our soul, we meet spirits from many levels of soul evolution. When our spirit returns to its soul at our physical dying time, it is return-ing to its true self to become absorbed in the whole."

As she spoke I felt as if I was with someone who understood my words. I was no longer behind a sheet of glass. Up to that point I had thought that if I ever talked about my experience I would be considered insane. Betty didn't think I was insane. She was down-to-earth and practical and she had explained things to me clearly. What she said made sense and I believed her. I knew, in my heart, that she was telling me the truth as she knew it, as it had been revealed to her.

I felt infinitely relieved. It was as if she had reached out for my hand and was guiding me along a difficult path. We went on to talk about how I was going to 'recharge my bat-teries'. She pointed out that I needed a holiday. I suppose she saw this in the colour of my auric field but she didn't mention that.

"How much time can you take off?" she fired at me.

Together we sat and worked it out. I calculated that I could take a three-month sabbatical from my work. I had been left a small legacy by my father which I had invested. I decided that this was the moment to use the money. It was all I had, anyway. I felt that the time had come to invest this legacy in myself.

I left Betty's house feeling optimistic and lighter in my heart. I finally knew what had happened to me over those three days. What she said corresponded with what both Clare and Colette had discovered in my body at Middle Piccadilly. I had left my body, and I had returned to it. Now I needed to go away and reflect on the impact of all these experiences. I needed time to myself away from everyone and everything.

As I drove away from Betty's house I started to think about the best time to take three months off and where I would go during that period. For the first time in a very long while I began to see some sense in all the things that had happened to me. I began to glimpse some meaning in my world.

A few weeks after my appointment with Betty Balcombe, I had another long-standing appointment in my diary. This time it was to consult an astrologer, Melanie Reinhart. Melanie is no ordinary astrologer. I had read her book *Chiron and the Healing Journey* several years before and found it profoundly moving. I had no idea what had prompted me earlier in the year to ring her and make an appointment. I can only imagine that I was reaching out for some understanding of the turbulent process I was going through.

My fascination with astrology had started as a child. I have a cluster of planets in Aquarius, including the Sun. This, according to Melanie, made me a 'super-Aquarian'. Aquarians tend to live in the future. I did so as a child. The present was too difficult and painful a place to be and so I would look up at the stars and imagine that I would find some meaning, some understanding for my life, by engaging with the heavens. I suppose the seeds of my deep respect and affection for astrology were sown in that childhood.

A horoscope, or natal chart, is a map drawn of the position of the planets in the heavens at the particular time, day and place of one's birth. This map can then be interpreted by an astrologer. It is an extraordinary experience to have a complete stranger describe one's essential character from a map of the heavens!

Over the years, astrology had helped me to understand myself, who I was, how I operated in the world and in relationships, and to accept myself with all my flaws, frailties and strengths. I was very attracted not only to the symbology of the chart but also to the psychological insight it provided. The elements of water, fire, earth and air spoke to my imagination. The planets Venus and Mercury, Saturn and Mars, Jupiter and Neptune, Uranus and Pluto enthralled me. The life of the Sun and the Moon and the Ascendant danced vividly before my eyes. Each one in its own way had helped me to get to know myself a little better.

My first birth chart was drawn up when I was in my twenties. In my thirties I worked closely with an astrologer for a period of three years. I attended a study course but couldn't find the magic of the heavens in the formal lectures. That was not astrology as I knew it and after that I continued to study informally, drawing up the charts of friends and family in order to get the practical experience I needed to extend my knowledge. I gave up astrology when I became a counsellor. Somehow astrology and person-centred counselling didn't make comfortable bedfellows. But here I was again having my chart drawn up at another critical point in my life.

I didn't tell Melanie about my abortion or my spirit child. I had started to feel better in myself over the previous couple of weeks. At Middle Piccadilly and in talking to Betty, I had found people with whom I could share my experience and I no longer felt so alone. I had improved a lot after my visit to Betty who had been so matter-of-fact about my out-of-body experiences.

Melanie started by talking about what it meant for me to be an Aquarian, about my strong sense of ideals and beliefs and about Aquarius being a bridge-building sign because it contains the urge to go beyond what is known to build something productive. "There is a very powerful visionary streak in you and also a strong desire to make an impact, make a difference, do something useful. I feel you are the sort of person whose wish to make a contribution outweighs the discomfort of the fact that whatever manifests will never quite measure up to the purity and clarity of the original vision.

"I don't think I'm exaggerating when I say that there is a very fundamental change going on here" she continued, looking at the chart in front of her. "What I imagine is happening, as you have several planets in air, is that there is a grinding down and eventual transformation of your most fundamental beliefs. You are going through a time of breakdown of ideals, beliefs and principles against which you have measured your sense of self-worth. Some of these expectations and principles no longer serve you because they come from your family of origin and are no longer true to who you are as a person or where you want to go in your life. So there is a struggle to transform and to realign your deepest values and this can be very painful as you pull away from the past. It is also very painful because it means that for a time you won't have that sense of vision. When that light goes out, the world can be a very depressing place."

"Well," I said, "I have been feeling as if I'm wandering around in the darkness. My world has been very, very dark."

"During this period, and for another year or so, there is a very profound change going on and very deep insight, quite literally, into how you think about things, what 'IT' is all about, who you really are and so on. From your earliest childhood some aspects of your nature were excluded. These aspects have felt exiled and part of your present psychological work is to bring those parts of yourself back home, back into yourself."

How strange that she should use those very words 'back home' when only two weeks before I had been talking to Betty about not knowing where 'home' was any longer. Melanie was using those words as if 'home' was *inside me*, not somewhere 'out there'.

But she was continuing and I wanted to hear everything she said. "It would be very useful for you to have some routine or habit of meditation to create space in your life for just BEING," she said. "There are a lot of powerful, dynamic aspects in your chart which are very much about DOING, taking action, helping others, wanting to be useful, but actually with your North Node in Aries in the twelfth house, the house of the hermit, of surrender, you need to allow the experience of the formless into you. You need to plumb the depths of your own inner experience. You need time for the realisation of your Being and I would guess from looking at your chart that this theme may be a major track on which your life runs from now on.

"With that North Node there is an impetus for a very profound spiritual journey. It's very strong in your chart and you need to allow yourself to be led, to have time alone, time to yourself, time to meditate, to be by the sea, to be in the mountains, time to drift and to dream, to reflect and to ruminate."

I felt tearful as she said this. It seemed like an impossible dream in my busy life. And yet I knew my heart yearned for those very things.

"There is probably a big taboo about being selfish," she said. "Yes... there seems to be a clear message: 'I must not be selfish.' There is, however, such a thing as 'enlightened selfishness' which is about being able to regenerate, restore and nourish yourself sufficiently in order to be of service in the world. You can't leave yourself out of the picture.

"Next year," she said, "Uranus and Neptune will powerfully stimulate your Ascendant and a new picture of who you are will emerge. There will be an awakening of a new impulse to action, a new perspective will develop... "

"But I feel in such a fog NOW," I said. "I have no sense of vision any more. I can't describe my experience in logical, rational ways. I'm often at a loss for words... "

"Well", she said, "I want to talk about that because it's to do with Mercury. Your Mercury is in Capricorn in the ninth house. The ninth house is the house of vision, of the higher mind, of the human search for meaning. Mercury is the planet of communication. Capricorn is a highly structured earth sign. There are some extremely powerful transits keying right in to your Mercury. Things in Capricorn take a long time to change. It's the densest of the Earth signs which is why it's so productive. However, when there is a process of change afoot that you haven't planned, that's the worst Capricorn nightmare.

"At the moment there are two big outer planets, Neptune and Uranus, conjunct in Capricorn. This is a big deal. It only happens every 171 years! And they are sitting right on top of that Mercury. It's like being on a promontory of earth stuck way out in the sea, getting pounded by the waves. You can't see what's going on. This has been happening all year but there was a turning point in the last week of September. I don't know if you felt that in any way...?"

"All I know is that I started to feel better, lighter..." I said, thinking of the lightness of heart I had felt when I left Betty's house.

"That'll do," Melanie said and we laughed together.

"My whole body has felt as if it was burning," I said.

"Yes, that makes sense because the changes in Capricorn seem to be permeating into a very physical level which includes one's body, one's job. It's not just an abstract change, it's for real. The maximum churning for you would have been April to September."

I didn't say anything out loud, but I thought to myself, "Yes, that fits exactly with what has been going on."

"I wouldn't be surprised if that fog doesn't also consist of a great deal of fear," she said.

I remembered the fear that had awoken me every night for months. "Yes, I have been feeling intensely afraid."

"Well, if you are feeling the fear, that is very positive. If you are feeling fear, then things are really moving. Having the fear in your field of awareness is very healing. How have you worked with that fear?"

"I wrote poetry," I replied.

"That's excellent because the transit to your Mercury is directly connected to your Moon in Pisces which is the very essence of flow and feeling: wordless and formless... so things are really happening if you are writing poetry!"

"I feel so verbally exhausted that poetry is like cool water running over my hot body," I said.

"Well, it doesn't surprise me that you should say that, because the body is also a place of renewal for you. You need to immerse yourself in matter, you need to go back to your body, to be surrounded by nature and allow yourself to let nature renew you and nourish you. There is a very profound mind-body connection being stimulated and when one is exhausted you must renew yourself by moving into the other. Have you thought about having a massage?"

I thought of my visit to Middle Piccadilly, which had been all about renewing and nourishing my body, and felt amazed at how I had intuitively known what I needed.

"Now," she said, "I'm looking at your planets in earth signs, and I feel that a whole new manner of verbal self-expression is sitting there, ready and waiting to emerge, but it may need time in order to do so. Things in earth work best when they are given time. Mercury needs time to coagulate its words out of a formless mass of feeling and that can't be hurried. Mercury is like the servant of the Sun. In your chart, he is a good servant, very devoted, full of integrity and very inspired, but he is slower than the master would like!

"One last thing," she said. "I think it would be very good for you at this time to seek out like-minded people, to have your ideals or deepest feelings about society confirmed in some way. Aquarians are very concerned with groups and group consciousness and it is important for you to be with people who respect your values, people with whom you have a mental resonance... not necessarily who share and uphold your values but who can give you the space without attacking or disparaging you in any way, because it's possible that in your early life your heartfelt idealism did come under attack..."

Tears filled my eyes again. My heart was touched by the warmth in her voice when she spoke to me in that way. I knew that I had found it hard as a child to have my belief in the essential goodness of humanity ridiculed and scorned. It had become easier as I grew older. I had continually banged up against or been confronted by things that had shattered those ideals and I had begun to understand life from a much broader perspective.

The consultation ended shortly after that and I drove home. I knew I would listen to the tape of the session many times. I marvelled at how, yet again, the language and symbolism of astrology had been able to provide a structure and a meaning to my experience. I felt comforted by the session with Melanie. It was familiar territory at a time of travelling through unknown lands in so many other ways.

The weeks passed and I thought a great deal about my sessions with Betty and Melanie. The astrological consultation had been the psychological equivalent of talking to my osteopath. It helped me to understand more clearly what was happening. It wasn't that I felt better, but I had found the meaning of my experiences. I could work with that! Now I wanted to think about how to integrate the information they had given me into my life.

In the meantime, I noticed that the way I was working as a counsellor had started to change. Not only was I talking far less in the sessions than I had done previously but I had started to have very clear pictures in my mind when I was with certain people — pictures that were to do with my clients' past experiences. I found that if I shared those impressions with my clients, something shifted very profoundly in the session.

I also noticed that I started to have very hot hands with some clients. Moreover, I would get a very strong sense of wanting to place my hands or direct the energy that I could feel in them towards a specific place on their bodies. At first, I kept this to myself. Then I realised that if I kept this to myself I would get a splitting headache after the session.

I rang Betty and asked her what to do. She suggested that I was starting to transmit healing energy to others. She said it was important that I should do so or the energy would build up. "Just talk about what's happening to you if you don't want to touch a person," she said. "Even talking about what you are feeling will release the energy. But remember that you must always close the energy down afterwards and work right through the energy centres from the crown to the feet."

It happened that I had a few new clients at this time and with them I was able to be quite free with the new abilities that were coming through to me. I began to develop my work as a channel for healing energies. I started to learn about the chakras and the subtle bodies. However, I felt deeply inhibited with the clients with whom I had worked for several years and often remained silent at the cost of a severe headache!

I had a strong urge to return to Middle Piccadilly. My logical mind said that I still had several weeks' worth of drops from Clare and that I should wait until I had finished my bottle but my intuitive mind was insistent and seemed to be saying, "Go now! Trust yourself! Follow your heart!" I was learning to trust the more intuitive side of myself, so with slight trepidation I booked myself in for another stay. I was allocated the room called 'Bluebell'.

The journey was a familiar one this time and I enjoyed it more. I knew what to expect; I knew the people who would be giving me the treatments. I still felt quite shy, however, and was mortified when the very first thing that happened to me on that second visit was that I broke a large white dish! I was so upset. I'm usually very careful and rarely break things but this platter just slipped through my fingers as I was drying it after the evening meal. Next morning's treatment with Colette shed light on the incident.

After my aromatherapy massage Colette told me that she felt she had again been doing past life work. "This time I felt as if your hands had been cut off," she said. "I felt the energy returning to them as I was massaging them."

I told her about breaking the plate the night before and how I had felt as if I had no hands with which to hold the plate. That incident made more sense to me now. I also told her how I was beginning to use my hands in my work.

"My hands are beginning to get very hot when I'm with clients" I said, "and I remember them being like this when I was a child. I would lie in bed in the mornings with these hot, hot hands, and my fingers feeling very swollen, as if they were giant sausages. I can still remember what it felt like even after all this time."

"Well," said Colette, "I felt the energy returning to your hands as I worked on them. I felt as if I was connecting them up to your arms again and I worked hard to do so."

"What else has happened since the last session we had?" I asked.

"A lot has shifted. I feel that you are beginning to give birth to yourself with the processes you are going through. Your energy levels are a bit better, enabling the kidneys to release the blocked fear and shock. The shock was based in the kidney and stomach areas."

"What oils have you used this time?" I asked her.

"This time I used Lavender again, to heal, especially the whole throat area (throat chakra). I also used Melissa for the shock and Sweet Orange for the stomach (solar plexus) area for nourishment and warmth. The throat healing relates to your need to express yourself. You have been very held in in your throat since you were a baby and you need to release the energy in that area. I feel you need to express *yourself*, to find and to make your own sound.

"The smell of the oils mixed together was metal and earth. This indicates that the grief is still releasing itself but that there is also a need to start to nurture yourself."

Again after the aromatherapy treatment I slept all afternoon. There was something about this place that just made me want to sleep! I was overcome with exhaustion, the deep exhaustion of grief and profound change. Here, in this haven of peace, I could let go and surrender to it.

The next morning I had my second consultation with Clare. I started by saying, "I know I haven't finished the second bottle you gave me but I just have this strange feeling that I *had* to see you."

Clare laughed. "I'm not surprised," she said. "I've just returned from a trip where I got a whole lot of new essences. You probably need some of them right away!"

I was amazed. She wasn't angry or irritated. She didn't feel I was bothering her or any of the things that I thought she might think. She accepted that if I was there it was because I needed to be there. My heart softened, and I relaxed. I realised how tense I had been, thinking she would disapprove of my visit.

We went through the same procedure as the last time. I placed my finger on the top of a bottle and Clare gently rested her hand over my finger. In her other hand she held the pendulum. I watched in fascination as it swung round and round and she picked out five bottles.

As she lined them up, she told me about each essence. Yet again I was astonished at the accuracy of the choices. She gave me my remedy bottle and instructed me to take two drops morning and evening for three months. I asked her if she would write all the information down for me so that I could keep it as a record of my health and healing. Included with the notes on the flower and gem essences was Clare's case study of the session.

Isabella reported that the first remedy combination was working. She felt that for the first time in her life she was able to listen to her spirit before anything else, which has required adjustment from all those around her. Whilst allowing herself to be emotionally fragile, she was able to go through the transition process without blocking herself. It is the start of her spiritual journey. She was experiencing headaches and overload due to having to use her analytical skills in her psychotherapeutic work. She was also experiencing lower back pain as the mental structures that no longer served her new perception of herself worked their way out through her muscular system.

The remedies she chose were:

Amethyst, *a Pegasus gem essence which is primarily for the tension-type headaches and to alleviate the pressure-cooker build-up in her head. Amethyst helps in the intense period that can occur just before a big shift and time of transition. It is a soul stone to aid the ability to listen to the dictates of her soul.*

Pink Seaweed, *a Pacific Sea essence, is a grounding remedy for patience before new beginnings, to help harmonise her thoughts before taking any action into something new, to shift out of the comfort zone into the new and the challenging, softening resistance to change and allowing the change to happen with grace and ease.*

Silver Princess, *an Australian Bush essence, is for unclarity in direction and purpose in life, for feeling aimless and despondent. It will help to give her life purpose, direction and motivation.*

Psyche, *an Amazon Orchid essence from the Andreas Korte essences, helps to enhance self-knowledge, understanding and inspiration by accessing the past life stream of consciousness to retrieve lost skills and stored knowledge. This essence will help her to open up on the whole psychic level especially for her trip to South America, the Andes, to reconnect with her spiritual roots.*

IUG Kenya 333, is a Gem essence for protecting Isabella as she goes through the whole process of change. It will also help to protect her from the emotional and mental negativity that she has a tendency to absorb from her clients.

The essences prescribed were for the spiritual awakening and rebirth of her true self initially instigated by the abortion and the relationship with her spirit child thereafter. Through these processes, Isabella is re-empowering herself as a woman.

I returned from my second visit to Middle Piccadilly with a new sense of purpose. My intuition told me that it was absolutely right to be going there and working with the therapies they had to offer, although they were so different from anything I had previously encountered. I felt as if I was with people who understood and accepted me at a very deep level and who were there to help me on my spiritual journey.

I began, tentatively, to feel full of wonder at the world that was opening up to me through the birth of my spirit child. I felt a tremendous broadening of my awareness as I allowed myself cautiously to approach the world of the intangible. I sensed a subtle higher plane that was accessible to my consciousness.

"I wonder if I will ever see you again?" I said out loud one day to my spirit child. If I closed my eyes, I could still picture her as a small, newborn baby as I had seen her on that summer's morning.

CHAPTER EIGHT

And I did see my spirit child again. This time she visited me in a dream, not long after my return from that second visit to Middle Piccadilly. I didn't realise it was her at first.

I had decided to take three months off, following my consultations with Betty and Melanie. Both of them, in their own way, seemed to be saying that I would benefit from time to myself, time to recharge, to regenerate. I also felt I really needed a holiday and to get away from everything familiar to me, so that I could retreat into myself. I needed time to integrate all the changes that had happened in my life and work — to think and reflect, unhampered by commitments.

My destination was Chile in South America. Chile had fascinated me since I was a child. It is a strange country, 2500 miles long and yet no more than 100 miles wide, bordered by the Andes to the east and the Pacific Ocean to the west. One of only two countries in South America not to have a border with Brazil. Cut off and remote. Full of volcanoes. It is said that the fishermen out on the Pacific Ocean can see sparks from the volcanoes in the night sky along the mountain skyline.

There was another reason that I wanted to go to Chile. For many years I had travelled to and from Argentina. It was my birthplace and my family still lived there. When I boarded the plane in Buenos Aires, there were always some passengers already on the aircraft. They had boarded in Chile where the flight originated. And when I returned to Buenos Aires, a small group of passengers always remained on board to continue the flight to its very end, Chile. These people and their destination intrigued me. I realised that I wanted to be one of those passengers who boarded the flight at the very beginning or remained on the flight to the very end! And so it was that I decided to travel to Chile on my sabbatical. I booked my flight: London–Buenos Aires–Santiago de Chile–Buenos Aires–London.

It was in the weeks before my departure that my spirit child visited me for the second time. She came to me in a dream. I drew the dream in a series of pictures. But I realised that drawing it wasn't enough. I wanted to talk about it. I wanted to immerse myself in the dream again and hear what my spirit child was saying to me. So I booked a consultation with a transpersonal psychotherapist with whom I had worked in the past and whom I trusted. She suggested that I go back into the dream, starting at the beginning, and that I talk from the dreambody.

"I will write down anything you say and you can take the notes home with you afterwards," she said.

And so, with the drawings of my dream spread out in front of me, I started to speak: "I am standing by this blue pram at the side of a road. The road goes either up the hill or down the hill. If I follow the road up the hill, it leads to a dark and forbidding castle. The castle is moated. Its windows are severe. It looks remote and frightening and grim. If I follow the road down the hill, it leads towards the town. The town is bustling, heaving with life. Radios are blaring, people are shouting, dogs are barking, children are crying. The town is alive with activity. The road only goes up the hill to the castle or down the hill to the town and I have to choose one of these two directions in which to push the pram. Both the castle and the town are familiar places to me. I know the road between them well. I don't want to go either way."

"So you don't want to go either up the hill or down the hill," she says.

"No, I don't. Then I notice the grass at the side of the road and beyond the grass I see an ancient forest. I hadn't noticed either the grass or the forest before. I realise that that is where I want to go. I don't want to go either up the hill or down the hill. I want to walk across the grass towards the great forest that I can see in the distance. I grip the handle of the pram, of my blue pram, and...

"I look ahead at the trees, the beautiful, ancient, magical trees and I think, 'It's too far; it's too risky and I can't do it. I can't leave the road behind me. I can't leave all those familiar things. Those familiar things and people and places that give my life structure and stability. That give my life warmth and noise, activity and meaning. They *are* my life, and I can't leave them.' I remain paralysed at the side of the road; knowing that I don't want to stay on the road but not knowing how to step off it either.

"I hold the handle of the pram and look down at my sleeping child. It's my spirit child. She's four months old now. She's still sleeping. She's a warm bundle in the pram. I look up towards the trees. They seem a very long way off. A long way into unknown territory."

"What happens to you when you look ahead at the trees?" the therapist asks.

"When I look ahead at the trees, I feel terror. My body trembles and aches. I start to sweat with the fear I'm feeling. I want to vomit with fear."

"Do you know what that fear is about?" she asks again.

"Yes," I reply. "It's fear of the unknown, fear of the risks I'm taking, fear of what others will say. The trees look very far away. I know I shall never reach them. They are too far away."

I'm silent for a long time. "What are you doing now?" she asks.

"I'm looking down into the pram, at my sleeping child, and I'm feeling calm and still and peaceful. A great warmth is flooding into my heart. I want to step off the road and walk across the grass to those beautiful, magical, ancient trees. I want to say: 'Yes! This is the way I am meant to go! Yes! I can do it!' The warmth in my heart is filling me with hope. The warmth in my heart stills my fear. I grasp the handle of the pram with my two hands and I step off the road: the road that only goes either up the hill or down the hill. I step off the road and I can feel the cool grass under my bare feet. I look down into the pram. I look down at my magical child, my four-month-old magical child, and I focus all my attention on her, on this one moment. I am living in this moment in time and only in this moment, and this moment is followed by another moment. I live in this present moment and I look at her as I'm pushing the pram. I'm not going to look up to see where I'm going. I'm looking at her. I focus all my attention on her small face on the pillow and on her small body asleep in the pram. And as I do so, the warmth in my heart spreads throughout my body.

"And I am slowly, slowly pushing the pram onto the grass. Off the road and onto the grass, one step at a time. I mustn't look up at the trees or I will be filled with fear again. I must keep looking at my sleeping child. And that is what I do. I am walking, step by step, over the grass, not looking into the distance at my destination, but looking down into the pram, down into my heart, and I find that I have the courage and the peace and the strength to walk forwards after all. Yes! I am walking towards the forest and my four-month-old baby is still asleep in her pram."

"How are you feeling now?" the therapist asks.

"As I walk towards the trees, pushing the blue pram, I am enjoying this feeling of adventure, this setting off on an undiscovered track. I relax as I walk, I drop my shoulders and begin to breathe deeply. And as I walk towards the trees, I'm beginning to realise that *where* I'm going is not as important as I thought it was. What is important is that I'm walking, that I'm walking and pushing the pram and feeling the warmth in my heart. What is important is that I'm relaxed and happy and even a little carefree! I'm not frightened any more. In fact I'm enjoying my freedom."

"You're enjoying your freedom!" she echoes.

"Yes! I'm free. I have left the road and I'm free!" I exclaim. "My spirit child has helped me to be free!"

The session was over. The therapist handed me the pages of notes. I thanked her, paid and left.

I was very excited by this dream. I was excited that my spirit child had come to me again. She was alive and growing and I felt she had chosen this moment to appear in order to help me learn something about myself. I didn't think it was a coincidence that she had appeared to me just as I was planning to 'step off my familiar road'. It seemed that, just as Melanie had said, the old structures, the old foundations, were falling away and from this dream I could see how full of fear I was about the crumbling of the old but also how ready I was to risk a new path.

During this time of lack of focus and centre, the image of holding on to the handle of the pram and looking down at my sleeping child gave me an inner strength. The road going up the hill or down the hill symbolised for me the feelings and emotions I had outgrown, the old structures of my life that no longer served me. I realised I would have to ride the tides of confusion, insecurity and uncertainty before the new became more distinctly defined.

I held my child and the dream in my heart while I was away travelling. I felt that new opportunities were opening up for me with the greater awareness I was developing of the realm of intangibles, the realm of the Divine. I felt she was saying to me, "Look, I am sleeping peacefully. I trust you to take care of me. Now you need to trust yourself. You need to trust your inner child who lives in your heart. Follow your heart and it will help you merge with something greater than yourself. Follow your heart and you will find your own inner light!"

The three months that I took off helped me greatly. By expanding my physical horizons through travelling to a new country, I was given the opportunity to have my mind opened, and my eyes too, to different lifestyles and attitudes towards living. I met and associated with people who had unusual ideas, who lived their lives in different ways to mine and I felt expanded by the experience of meeting them. Expanded and challenged! Many of my rigid structures, values and ideals started to crumble as I became aware of how conservatively I had lived my life.

I felt that this period spent travelling deepened my understanding both of the experiences I had had with the birth of my spirit child and of the new levels of awareness I had gained in my work. I felt freer to explore new realms. I saw that my previous structures could be used as a foundation, a springboard to new horizons. I started to discover that the very act of asking the big questions had begun a process of self-discovery and self-knowledge that was to be invaluable.

By the time I returned home I was ready to change and to introduce new ideas and habits into my life. I started to set aside time to meditate every day. I had begun to meditate while travelling and found that, as Melanie had suggested, I relished the inner space it gave me. I felt more centred and calm. At first I wondered how I would manage it in a house where the children had always had direct access to me and where I had imposed few boundaries around my personal time. I enlisted my son's help by asking him to make me a sign for my door. It read: MEDITATING. DO NOT DISTURB!

The first time I pinned it to my door I thought the children would fall about laughing. I felt self-conscious and shy and ready to be ridiculed. But nothing happened! The telephone rang. What should I do? I realised that I didn't have to answer it simply because I was in the house. I let the answerphone take the call. I introduced my meditation time as a period when I was totally unavailable to everyone and everything. And we all survived!

Slowly I incorporated the discipline of meditating into my everyday life. I would set aside time in the morning and the evening for stillness. Sometimes I would sit with my journal next to me and when I finished my meditation I would pick up my crayons and draw whatever came into my mind. At other times, I would write down any words that came into my head. I found that this practice connected me to a core of warmth inside me. I felt calm, peaceful and expanded by the experience. I started to discover things about myself that I had had a glimpse of when Helena Rose visited me for the second time and I felt I was anchoring what I had glimpsed in my daily life in a very practical way.

In the summer I took to meditating outside. It was lovely. I would sit under the silver birches and feel my connection with nature renewed. I sensed the oneness with all living things that I had felt when my spirit child was born. I was able to recapture some of the feelings and sensations of lightness and lovingness that had surrounded me. The children came to accept my meditation discipline as part of the family routine.

My little grove of silver birches had grown. On my return from Chile I had felt a deep need to plant a tree for my spirit child. I knew exactly which tree I wanted to plant. It was a Robinia Frizia. It has pale golden leaves, feathery and oval in shape, borne on long graceful branches. In autumn the leaves turn beautiful shades of red and orange before they fall to the ground.

I bought the tree on Easter Sunday and brought it home with great care. I sat in my garden with the tree next to me and wondered where to plant it. It was some time before I knew where it had to go and then I wondered why it had taken me so long to decide! This was one of the changes that was happening inside me. I was finding it more and more difficult to make decisions in a logical and rational manner. I had to wait until the right decision emerged from my heart and that took time. I often felt impatient and frustrated. I chuckled at how accurate Melanie's chart reading had been. How difficult it was for me to give myself time to allow things to emerge from a formless mass of feeling!

However, I was rewarded for my patience with the knowledge of the exact place to plant the Robinia. It came to me early one morning after my meditation. I had been sitting under the silver birches and I realised that they formed a triangle. If I planted the tree in a certain place, the four trees together would form a kite shape. That seemed fitting. The three silver birches were my three children on this earth plane and the Robinia Frizia was my fourth child, on the spirit plane.

Later that week, my son and a friend dug a large hole. We watered the ground and planted the tree and welcomed it into the garden. We stood around and looked at it: this tall, rather spindly brown stick with a few twigs sticking out from the top of it! Would it ever grow? I thought it unlikely. But I was wrong. It did grow. I watched it. In the spring it seemed to take a very long time to produce any leaves compared to all the other trees around it. But slowly, slowly, the twiggy branches lengthened and thickened. Small pale yellow shoots appeared which turned into feathery leaves. It really began to look like a tree!

A few weeks later Vincent came to lunch. He looked out at the garden and said, "You've planted a tree."

"Yes," I replied. Should I tell him why I had planted it? What would he say? Would he understand? Did I want him to know?

"I planted a tree for our child," I said. And in saying those words the tears came. His tears and my tears. We held each other.

"Take me to the tree," he said.

So we went out to the garden and stood by the tree. He stood one side and I stood the other side. We stood together and we cried together and then we held each other and I opened my heart again. I anchored the love I felt for my unborn child and her father into the earth. I let the tears flow into the earth, healing tears, joyful tears.

"You see, I have planted her just a little way off from the other three trees," I explained.

"Yes," he replied.

"I wanted them to be separate and different but together," I added, just in case he didn't understand what I meant.

"Yes," he said.

And so the tree joined the little grove of trees in my garden. It wasn't quite the forest I had seen in my dream, but I felt that I had reached a destination nonetheless.

Later that summer, I found myself walking into a shop where a medium and clairvoyant did readings. I don't know what made me go in. I had never noticed this shop before, although I had walked past it often. This time, however, I walked in and looked around me at all the books on spiritual matters and the crystals and the cards that lined the shelves.

"Those shelves are rather dusty," I thought to myself, ever practical and down-to-earth. Despite the dust, I liked the feeling in the shop. I asked about having a reading. I was told

I could have a reading there and then or make an appointment for another day. There and then felt a little too soon for me, so I left the shop. I was cautious and wanted to go home and think about it before I committed myself to a reading with a medium! As the days passed, I felt more and more strongly that it was important to have a reading, so I rang the shop and made an appointment.

The medium spoke at length about several events in my life and I found myself feeling very still and serene while she talked. She could see the suffering I had been through and her empathy touched me deeply. Suddenly she asked me a question:

"Do you have a child in spirit?"

"A child in spirit? What do you mean?"

I was flustered by the question. I hadn't expected it.

"Well, I have a child in spirit here with me now and she wants me to say to you that you mustn't be sad that she is no longer with you. She wants me to say to you that her purpose was only to stay for a short time. She only needed a touch of life. Your purpose is to stay for longer. You have work to do in the world and her purpose was to help you with that work. She's saying, 'My work is done. Do not regret what happened. It is as it should be.'" The medium was in a slight trancelike state now. I felt dreamy myself. Dreamy, serene and peaceful.

"She wants to give you a gift," said the medium. "She's laying them out before you. She's giving you a gift of a prayer book, a poem and a rose. They are for you. I can see them clearly."

Tears filled my eyes. And then, all of a sudden, I felt her presence in the room, this small room in this weird shop under the arches. I felt her presence as I had done when she was born and when she came to me in my dream. She was here in the room with me. I knew it even though I couldn't see her. A warmth flooded into my heart as I opened up to her loving presence. I felt a tingling sensation on my skin, a feeling of being wrapped in a warm summer's breeze, light and gentle, soft, baby soft.

I don't remember how I left the shop. I never went there

again. There was no need to. I knew why I had had to go there. So much of what the medium had said affirmed my own sense of why my spirit child had come to me and why I had chosen to have an abortion. I found it extraordinary that this unknown woman could have told me so many things about my life that made such sense to me. I spent the rest of the day walking. I thought about the world that had opened up to me over the past year. I walked and I thought and I reflected on my changing self. I wondered whether I looked different on the outside too.

I returned to Middle Piccadilly again and again. It was part of my healing journey and a place where I learnt more and more about a different way of being and working with people. The knowledge and information they offered helped me in my work in groups and with clients. My work expanded as I began to trust my intuition and my Higher Self.

I realised how rigid I had been in my outlook, how conservative. I was no longer sure of what I thought about anything. I kept wanting to order my thoughts but I found that any attempt at structuring had a very negative effect on my physical health. My headaches would return and my neck would stiffen up.

At times I found it difficult to express what was on my mind as my thoughts seemed so complex and disordered. I discovered that I was becoming very receptive to subtle influences around me. My intuition became very sharp and I encountered in myself previously hidden psychic and healing abilities. I realised that I had lived, until the moment of the birth of my spirit child, in my head, in my mind. I now wanted to live in my heart and from my heart. This deepening experience of life affected everything around me. No longer were my actions and decisions based on logic alone. I started to trust my intuition. I began to understand the web of life that we all create — how every thought and word and deed have an impact on that web. New insights were coming into my life every moment. It was a profound and crucial period of change.

I felt as if I was starting to integrate some of what I had learnt when I had returned to my soul state. I began to grasp the workings of a Higher Order of which I had been completely unaware until that moment in time. I was waking up and becoming aware, really aware, of the world I lived in. Not only the physical world that I could see, touch, smell, taste and hear but also the unseen world that runs parallel to it.

I began to understood that every person who came into my life and every event that happened in my life had something to teach me by bringing up to the surface previously unknown aspects of myself. I often thought of Melanie and her words to me about 'bringing all sides of me back home'. I felt I was doing that, but the changes were so intense, so profound, so concentrated, that their meaning often did not make sense to me until time had passed.

My children would say, "You're not going to Middle Piccadilly again, are you?"

"Yes, I am," I would answer. It became my priority to heal myself and to find out my purpose for being here on Planet Earth. The death and birth of my daughter, my spirit child, had ensured my initiation on the soul's path.

One day I woke up and the early-morning sun was shining through my east-facing bedroom window. I could hear the birds singing in the trees outside. I could feel the heat of the summer sun, although it was still early. It was going to be another hot day. I lay dozing in my bed and suddenly I realised that it was my spirit child's birthday.

"Happy birthday, Helena Rose. You are one year old today," I said to her. "I wonder if you can hear me?" The question was irrelevant. I knew she was there.

Later that day, I lit a candle. The candle burned all day and in the evening I took it down and placed it under the tree I had planted for her. I watched it burn into the night, the starlit night.

CHAPTER NINE

I saw her again today. I heard a child's voice saying, "Daddy, Daddy, come... see." I looked around to see who had called. And then I saw her.

She was almost two years old. She held onto Vincent's hand and was pulling him towards a dandelion she had seen in the grass. He had been looking the other way. At the sound of her clear child's voice he turned, laughing, his face smiling and full of love. He turned around and allowed himself to be dragged by her insistent little hand. She strained her whole infant's body to pull him over, to show him the dandelion in the grass. Flaming yellow flower which fascinates me and was fascinating her. I saw them both bend down low over the flower. She pointed her fat little finger to the centre, the very centre of the flower. She plucked out a flower petal and observed it carefully. She held it between her thumb and forefinger, turning her hand round so she could see all sides of it.

I can see them both now in my mind's eye: father and daughter. Father laughing, happy, carefree, letting himself be pulled along by his daughter: serious, adorable golden curls framing her face. She was wearing a little white dress with pink frills, white socks and brown shoes. "Daddy, Daddy, come... see."

I hadn't seen her for a long, long time and the sight of her brought a lump to my throat and tears to my eyes. My heart filled with warmth and love. Child of my heart, child of the great Spirit, child who changed my whole life by her death and her birth. Why had she come again in this way into my life? What was she doing here? And why had she chosen to visit me again now?

I had been lying on a deck chair in the garden on a late spring afternoon, waiting for my children to return from school. My practice was finished for the day. I hadn't expected to see her ever again and hadn't recognised this child who was running around the garden. It took me several moments to realise that it must be my spirit child, Helena Rose. How she had grown! The last time I had seen her she had been a small baby in a pram and now here she was, almost two years old and walking and running and laughing and saying a few words. Why had she come with Vincent? I hadn't seen him either for a long time, not since the day when I had shown him the tree in the garden. I felt very shaken by her appearance.

The months had passed and my work had continued to expand, change and develop. I often felt attuned to universal and cosmic levels of being which had confused me at first but which I now found spiritually inspiring. The intense and crucial period of change had settled down and I was in the process of rebuilding my life, incorporating into it the realms of the intangible, the mystical. I hadn't seen my spirit child again and she had receded in my mind as other things had come to the fore. It wasn't that I wanted to forget about her but I did want to put the past behind me and the past meant both her and her father. And yet here they both were, together in the garden. What did it mean?

From that afternoon onwards, she didn't leave me. I couldn't get her out of my mind. She became a vivacious presence in my life. It seemed that every time I shut my eyes I saw her again. Every time I listened I heard her again. I could hear her laughter and her child's voice saying, "Daddy, Daddy, come... see." Her presence surrounded me. I couldn't sit in the garden without being acutely aware of her. I couldn't look at a dandelion, a flower I love, without seeing her bending down to gaze at it intently. I thought of her constantly and I saw her everywhere.

After several days of her haunting, uninvited presence I decided to take action. I welcomed her into my daily meditation time. It wasn't difficult to do as she was constantly around me anyway. After my initial invitation she would sit with me while I meditated. Day after day we sat together. I stopped questioning her reappearance in my life and began to accept her presence once again. In fact, I began to enjoy her companionship.

She accompanied me wherever I went, as one would take a two-year-old with one wherever one goes! I started to enjoy her delight in the world, at all the things she was doing and seeing. She seemed to be eternally curious and full of joy. I began to get to know her, this child of mine, conceived in love and bringing love into my life once more. I began to get to know her and to love her.

I was soon holding conversations with her! She seemed to speak to me, pointing things out to me that I hadn't noticed before, ordinary things, little things. She noticed everything around her. I was full of wonder at the way she was so spontaneous, so full of life. I found myself imitating her and in doing so I started to experience life much as a two-year-old might! I became more joyful and spontaneous as I went about my daily activities. I began to delight in the magic of my world.

I found myself talking to the vegetables in my refrigerator. "Well, which one of you wants to be cooked for lunch today?" I would ask the carrots, the broccoli, the beans, the corn on the cob. And it seemed that certain vegetables fell into my hand as if offering themselves to me. I started to engage in a relationship with the vegetables as I washed and peeled them and cut them up. I disliked putting them into the boiling water. I thought I could hear them screaming.

I felt as if I was playing a game, but I also knew it was a game of great seriousness. I was learning something about the world I lived in, how I had previously lived in it and how I was choosing to live in it now. I became mindful and attentive to my every action in each moment. Life seemed full of richness and experience when I lived it in that way.

When I went into the garden to pick some flowers, I would ask the flowers: "Which one of you wants to come into the house with me?" I walked around the garden, stopping at various plants and waiting to hear an answer to my question. Sometimes I returned empty-handed as if it was not the right time or the right day to bring any of them inside. Other days I went back into the house with my arms full of blooms.

I talked not only to the flowers but also to the trees and the animal creatures in the garden. I didn't say the words out aloud. It wasn't as if I could have been overheard, but I directed the thoughts in my head towards the plants and creatures that I 'spoke' to. I did it deliberately and in full consciousness of what I was doing. I engaged with them as fully as if they were people with whom I was having a conversation. I noticed that I felt as if I was in a relationship with them, that in fact we were in relationship with each other and this added another dimension to my life.

I remembered that I had been like this as a child, talking to the trees, the flowers, the grass, talking to the spirit life in the unseen spirit world. I remembered spending hours and hours outside in our garden, wandering around, feeling at one with all nature's living things. I recalled Melanie Reinhart saying how I must bring the exiled parts of myself back home and her words began to make more and more sense. I didn't have to leave my body any longer in order to communicate with all living things. I became more and more sensitive to the living world: the rustle of the leaves, the nodding of the flowers, the gathering strength of the breeze, the vibrations that emanated from all living things. They all became forms of communication with the unseen world.

Why had I exiled these parts of myself as a child? What world had I entered that this feeling of Oneness with all creation had become irrelevant? What had I forgotten? Why had I allowed myself to forget? What magic had I allowed to slip out of my life as I grew into adulthood?

In my deepest being I knew why I had stopped doing all these things. I would have been ridiculed and scorned. My family would have laughed at me — and not only my family but others too. I imagined that this powerful connection with the world of spirit set me apart from others and I hadn't wanted to be set apart. I wanted to be the same as everyone else.

That was one of the most disturbing things for me about the whole experience with my spirit child. I thought to myself, "Here I am again. Something is happening in my life that's setting me apart from others." And I feared that in talking about her and her life I would again be ridiculed, disparaged. I had more to lose now. I was a mother, a counsellor with a busy practice and a tutor on several highly regarded counselling courses. What would everyone think of me if they knew about my spirit life and my spirit child?

I began to see that my spiritual journey, the one that Melanie had seen as 'a major track on which my life would run from now on' had indeed become the focus of my life.

I had returned to Chile. On my second trip I had worked with Chilean medicine women belonging to the Mapuche indigenous Indians. I had been a translator of their teachings for a group of North American women who were on a shamanic retreat in southern Chile. I had found many of the teachings fascinating. In particular, I resonated deeply with their connection to the natural world. We had spent time in a forest by some natural volcanic pools in the south of the country, as well as travelling on horseback high into the central region of the Andes. I had immersed myself in nature and felt renewed and regenerated by the experience.

So, when I returned to London from that second visit, I had followed a deep yearning to be amongst ancient trees and had taken to walking in Richmond Park several times a week. My dog, a Jack Russell called Daisy, and I had covered almost every inch of the park on our walks. I loved this activity and was astonished that I hadn't realised how accessible the park was to where I lived!

After Helena Rose's visit to me in my garden, I noticed that she started to come on these walks with me. I felt the presence of this little child trotting along beside me. Sometimes I consciously slowed my pace, imagining that my energetic stride would be too fast for her. And, in so doing, I started to become aware of other aspects of the park that I hadn't noticed when I had walked faster: the way the sunlight fell through the trees, the colour of the leaves, the smell of the damp earth, the call of the geese, the feel of the tree trunks under my hand as I touched the bark in passing. I started to BE more and DO less.

I would stop and look and smell the air, the earth, the leaves. I would bury my head in the fresh new bracken. I would breathe in the beauty of the land over which I walked and thank God for its magnificence. As my pace slowed, my experience of the park became richer, and as it became richer it deepened and reached a point in my heart that touched the very core of life within me, the very depth of my being. I felt, once again, as if I were one with the trees, one with the leaves, one with the damp earth and the bracken. I reconnected with the experiences I had had when Helena Rose was born. Magic entered my life all over again as I surrendered to the call, the pull, of the land over which I walked.

It must have been shortly after Helena Rose's second birthday, a day that I had consciously remembered and celebrated this year rather than letting it tumble into my life unexpectedly. She and I had set out for our walk in the park when our way was barred by a female deer who appeared out of the bracken and became very aggressive towards us. I realised that she must have a young fawn hidden in the bracken and turned to go another way. However, the deer ran alongside us until I turned and crossed the road again the way I had come. This meant that I had to remain in a part of the park that I had always thought was rather uninteresting. I was irritated by this. I had been looking forward to a very specific walk through the woods. I wanted to enjoy the sunlight through the leaves at this time of day and I knew that the geese and the swans would be on the lakes. However, there was no way I was going to be able to get past this female deer, so I left my known path and continued my walk, not really noticing where I was going. I walked in a wide circle and on my return sat under a tree overlooking the meadow.

As I sat there, I noticed that this tree made a different sound from the trees around it as the summer breeze blew through its leaves. I was curious and looking up I saw that, although at first sight it had appeared to be the same as the other trees, in actuality it was different and set apart. I enjoyed the sound of the tree in the summer afternoon as it murmured and sighed. Helena Rose sat beside me. She was trying to tell me something but I was still irritated and I didn't want to listen to her. I was listening to the sound of the singing leaves in the tree.

For three consecutive days, this incident repeated itself. I would set out in the direction in which I wanted to go, towards the forest and the lakes, but the female deer would leap unexpectedly and aggressively out of the bracken and run alongside me until I returned to the other side of the road. I was becoming more and more confused! It seemed as if the deer was trying to communicate something to me and I just wasn't 'getting it'. By the third day, however, I found I was actually enjoying my new walk. Although it took me through a part of the park that I had always thought would hold little interest for me, in fact that was not so. I discovered a small pond where I saw a heron standing immobile on one leg. I saw a family of ducks and because the pond was set apart from the main park there were fewer people around. I also enjoyed stopping under the 'singing' tree as I called it.

On the third day of my walk, I stopped under the tree again, the singing, sighing tree, and again Helena Rose sat beside me. This time I was more responsive to her attempts to speak to me. I realised she was trying to tell me something and I couldn't understand what it was. I couldn't hear her. Her lips were moving but no sound came out of them.

I thought she was saying something like, "Story, story," but I couldn't be sure. I wondered whether she was asking me to tell her a story. "Do you want me to tell you a story?" I asked her. She shook her head and ran off. The leaves rustled over my head as I sat under the tree, wondering what to make of her.

When I returned home after that walk on the third day, I didn't go straight into the kitchen as I usually did but I continued through the house to the small room at the back overlooking the garden. This small garden room had been my consulting room once. It now housed a computer. I sat down in front of the computer and turned it on. I sat looking at the blank screen.

I opened a new file. I typed the words 'Spirit Child' at the top of the page and under 'Spirit Child' I typed the words 'Healing the Wound of Abortion'. I had no plan. I didn't know what those words meant and I didn't know what I would do next. I was following an inner prompting, responding to a Divine call, and as I did so those words had come to me.

The next day, I returned to the garden room, turned on the computer and opened the file again. I had called the file 'Isa's book'. Isa is my childhood nickname and few people in this country know it or use it. Why did I want to reconnect with my childhood nickname? Was this another part of me that I had exiled and needed to call back home? 'Isa's book'... 'Spirit Child'... 'Healing the Wound of Abortion'... What would happen next? What would follow those words staring at me from the computer screen?

As I sat there in front of the screen, I started to write. I could hear the words in my mind, the words that I was writing. I saw them in my mind's eye even before they unfolded on the page in front of me. I started to write about my spirit child, my fourth child, conceived in love, killed at eight weeks and born at eight months and eight days.

I wrote for three whole days. For three whole days, I walked my walk, the new walk in Richmond Park, and returned home to sit in front of the computer and write. I wrote until I was exhausted, until I was 'written out'. I wrote until I couldn't hear any more words in my mind. I didn't notice mealtimes or bedtimes. I didn't notice my children or their friends. I was immersed in my story, her story. I was immersed in my inner world, in a deep, deep ocean of words, images and memories.

At the end of the three days, it was finished; it was all over. I was hardly aware of what I had written and had no idea why I had written it. I had simply obeyed some inner voice that cried out to be spoken through me. The words wrote themselves. They flowed through me and my fingers typed them onto the screen in front of me. All I had to do was to sit at my computer and open the file and the words emerged of their own accord. And then they stopped coming and I knew I had finished. I knew it was all over. That night I went to bed and slept like a baby, an exhausted and contented baby.

The next morning I awoke late. I was immediately aware that something was different. At first I couldn't put my finger on it. Then I realised with a shock what it was. Helena Rose hadn't appeared as I lay in my half-awake state. I had got so used to seeing her in my mind's eye as I emerged from sleep and this morning she wasn't there. I opened and closed my eyes, hoping I could make her appear. But I couldn't. I couldn't feel her presence in the room with me either. She had simply vanished.

She didn't appear when I went to my meditation place and she didn't appear when I went out to the garden. She didn't appear when I looked at the dandelions in the grass. The day passed with no sign of her. And the next day and the next. She had gone. She had vanished as unexpectedly as she had arrived. I missed her dreadfully. My heart ached with sadness. I didn't feel right without her at my side. I felt as if I had lost her all over again.

I turned to the story of the 'Spirit Child' that I had written as a way of reconnecting with her. I read and re-read what I had written. And as I did so an overwhelming feeling came over me of absolute peace, of absolute certainty, an inner knowing. I knew why she had come back. I knew why she had stayed as long as she had. I understood why she had visited me for this third time.

I realised what she had been trying to tell me in the park, why she had accompanied me everywhere. Suddenly the sun came out from behind a cloud and I was illuminated! She had been trying to tell me that I must write her story. That was the purpose of her visit.

"Story... story... " she had said in Richmond Park, pointing at herself while I sat under the rustling tree. She had said it over and over again. Of course, "story... story" meaning "Tell my story." That's what she had wanted me to do.

I read and re-read what I had written. It was a magical

tale, full of rich imagery and language. It was a very personal account of our relationship. It was her story and it was my story too. I knew it was not for the public eye — it was too personal for that — so I decided to print it out, wrap the pages in soft tissue paper and put 'Spirit Child' away in a safe place.

Towards the end of that summer, I added to her story. I had a powerful vision which remained so firmly in my consciousness that I decided to write it down to conclude the story of 'Spirit Child'. I called the vision 'Unclaimed'.

I can see them now, all these unclaimed children. They are there and they are here, floating in the ether like balloons, multicoloured balloons, with strings attached.

They float this way and that, hovering just above the surface of the Earth. I can see them. I can feel their presence.

They are waiting for their mothers to reach out and take hold of the string, their string, this golden thread that would anchor them to the world, to our world and to their world... their angelic realm.

They are waiting for their mothers to call out to them, to call out for them. "My child, my child, I remember you. Do you remember me? I am your mother."

And the child, so called, answers, "Yes, Mother, I remember you. I am older now and I remember you and love you still. I can see you. You can't see me but I can see you."

It is never too late to reach out for that thread, that golden thread, that will connect you to your spirit child. It is never too late to reach out and say, "Hello!"

It is never too late to claim our unborn children. The children that float, waiting in the ether, for us to anchor their life in ours.

Reach out, reach out your hand and touch the golden thread. Can you feel it between your fingers? Can you imagine your spirit child hovering, suspended in space, at the other end of the golden thread?

Just reach out, reach out your hand, let your fingers touch the golden thread, and your spirit child will do the rest.

The powerful image of the spirits of these unborn children hovering in the ether was very vivid for me. I couldn't understand why this vision had come but I was learning to trust the images I saw and so I wrote the vision down and left the understanding to emerge at a later stage. I didn't have long to wait.

That autumn I attended an international conference in London on the subject of 'Birthing Spiritual Healing'. It was organised by the Doctor/Healer Network to which I belonged. It was attended by doctors, healers, midwives, gynaecologists, obstetricians, counsellors and other complementary therapists from around the world. The lectures, demonstrations and workshops focused on holistic approaches to promote the care of the whole person in any aspect of pregnancy, labour and birth.

I had already attended a previous conference on 'Psychotherapy and Spiritual Healing', which had brought together professional healers, therapists and doctors. For the first time in a long time I felt at home within a professional body. I was working with a group of people who shared my values and ideals within the counselling/ psychotherapy profession. I was meeting with practitioners who understood healing and were integrating it and counselling into their work. I learnt a tremendous amount about my own work as a counsellor/healer and felt very supported and encouraged by listening to the experiences of others working in a similar field.

Up until that conference, I had felt as if I had to keep secret the ever-growing awareness of my life's spiritual dimension. I felt the conventional world of counselling might disapprove of me. The spiritual realm, by its very nature, is a world that can't be rationalised, intellectualised, explained or analysed and it was, therefore, regarded with suspicion, fear and caution.

The 'Birthing Spiritual Healing' conference opened with presentations from several of the international speakers. Their panel presentations would be followed by experiential workshops in the afternoon. I was particularly drawn to one of the speakers, Dr Dorothea von Stumpfeldt. She and I had met at the previous conference and we had recognised each other immediately — not from this life, I hasten to add! We both knew we had met before and had worked together as healers. I found it liberating to have my own sense of recognition affirmed by hers. She knew, as I knew, that we would continue to meet across incarnations as we followed our work. We were part of a sisterhood.

Dorothea is a doctor practising psychotherapy and healing in Germany. After completing her formal studies she continued to search for deeper explanations for illness and death than are taught in conventional medical schools. Her clients were her teachers, leading her to ever-deeper understandings of a nature that was personal and individual to themselves. She developed Emotional/Body Therapy which brings people into contact with their inner wisdom to reveal what happened to them in this or former lives. The process is relatively quick and incredibly potent and can relieve current and old emotional hurts of many kinds. I was greatly looking forward to hearing what she had to say on the subject of Spiritual Birthing.

I was sitting in the front row. I'm deaf in one ear and I wanted to make sure I could hear what everyone said. Three of the panel had made their addresses to the conference before I started to feel very light, almost lightheaded. I was entering a trancelike state. My spirit child was in the room with me. I could feel her presence at my side. She had become so familiar to me that I now knew exactly when she came close to me.

At that moment Dorothea said, "I can sense the presence of all the unborn babies in this room. I can feel them calling out to their mothers in this room. Can you feel their presence?" She had her eyes closed while she said this and spread out her arms towards the participants.

I could feel my spirit child urging me on. "Tell my story. You must tell my story, here, today, now." My heart was beating very fast. I started to feel very hot, hot and flushed. I could feel my blood pounding in my veins. I didn't know what to do. Should I stand up? Where was the microphone? What would others think of me? Would they think I was mad? I felt more and more uncomfortable and wished I could say to her,

"Go away! Go away and leave me alone! Not here. Not now. Not today. I'm not ready to speak about you."

But I didn't do any of those things. I looked around for the microphone. I saw it. Slowly and deliberately I walked over to it and said, "There's something I want to say following on from what Dorothea has said." And hesitantly, cautiously, I told the assembled conference the story of my spirit child. I don't know where the words came from. I just know that my spirit child was there with me and that I spoke of my relationship with her before the abortion and after the abortion. I talked about my experience of giving birth to her and how it had plunged me into an altered state of consciousness. I talked about the three times she had visited me in dream visions. I continued to speak as long as I felt inspired to, as long as my heart felt it was on fire. And only when the words no longer came to me did I cease speaking.

Another member of the panel stood up: Francoise Freedman, PhD. Francoise is a Cambridge-trained anthropologist who specialises in medical anthropology with a focus on social and cultural aspects of reproduction. She was inspired to work in this field through living with Amazonian Indian women. She founded 'Birthlight', an association in Cambridge dedicated to the improvement of each individual's experience of childbirth.

Francoise stood up and talked about her own experience of abortion and her birth experience nine months after the conception. She told the conference how her spirit child had grown up between her husband and herself until she was twelve years old, when she had left them to incarnate as one of Francoise's spiritual guides. She said that the experience of a 'phantom labour' after having an abortion is a well known fact in other cultures who are more attuned to the spirit world and grounded in their bodies.

I was overjoyed! My story was being understood! I wasn't scoffed at or ridiculed. My outpouring wasn't considered foolish nonsense. I wasn't being labelled insane or odd. What I had gone through was real. Not only was it real but others had gone through a similar experience.

I didn't hear about the afternoon's events until later. A colleague of mine attended the workshop entitled 'Dealing with bereavement after abortion or death of a child', which Dorothea and Dr Daniel Benor facilitated together. She told me how many of the participants in that workshop had reclaimed the connection with their spirit children. She told me how the workshop had been profoundly influenced by the events I had been a part of in the morning. I returned home overwhelmed by everything that had happened.

I opened the manuscript of 'Spirit Child' and read again the vision I had recorded several weeks previously and called 'Unclaimed'. It all made sense to me now. The startling events of the day had been revealed to me prior to the conference. This was the meaning of the vision I had had. It was a prophetic vision. The vision of women claiming their unborn spirit children, their spirit babies, had taken root in the practical everyday world of the conference. It had taken form. The golden threads had been grasped. At least some of the multicoloured balloons no longer hung suspended in the ether, unclaimed.

That conference marked the end of an old, outworn, outdated way of life for me. I had found a new way of expressing myself which came from the subtle higher plane now accessible to my consciousness. I knew in my heart that I was finally learning to listen to and communicate what I was hearing from the angelic realms.

After reading 'Unclaimed' one more time, I again wrapped the pages of 'Spirit Child' in the soft tissue paper. My eyes were brimming over with tears. I walked down to the end of my garden and stood by the tree that I had planted for my spirit child. I looked at the graceful branches full of soft green and turning-slightly-orange leaves and then I sat crosslegged under the tree. The earth felt damp beneath me and the smell of it in the autumn evening filled my lungs. I looked up and saw the evening star shining brightly.

The tears brimmed over, ran down my cheeks and watered the ground around the Robinia. Tears of joy and tears of sorrow and, mostly, tears of Love.

EPILOGUE

Writing this book has been like having this child after all.

It was conceived at dawn in the hot volcanic springs of the 'Termas Colinas' high up in the Chilean Andes in the shadow of the 'San Jose' volcano, and born at Findhorn in Scotland forty weeks later.

At six weeks I announced my pregnancy by sending out the proposal for this book to potential publishers. There was to be no abortion this time around.

At three months I signed a contract with Findhorn Press. The pregnancy was fully under way and there was no turning back now.

The fourth and fifth months of pregnancy were the hardest. It was summer and all the memories of that summer when my spirit child was born were reawakened.

In months six, seven and eight it was a joy to feel pregnant and creative. By the ninth month I was beginning to feel it was time to give birth to this child!

My spirit child is five years old now. The same age I was when I told the spirits surrounding me to go away and leave me in peace. This time I welcome them in my life.

I haven't seen my spirit child again but I feel her presence everywhere. She has become an angel.

In writing this book I picked up the coloured wools of the original story of 'Spirit Child' and these I have used to knit the garment that is now this book. As with all knitting there have been dropped stitches and changes of pattern as the garment has taken on an identity of its own. You may even find some threads still hanging loose...

Isabella M. Kirton
—November 1997

APPENDIX

ELIZABETH'S STORY

I had known Elizabeth for at least four years before she had her abortion. So when she told me that she was pregnant and had decided to have an abortion, I wanted to say to her: "Think carefully about this. Is it really what you want to do?" I thought, however, that my judgement would be more of a hindrance than a help and so kept silent. Knowing Elizabeth as a highly sensitive and intuitive person, I wondered how her body and mind would tolerate the trauma of abortion.

Elizabeth has generously agreed to tell her story in this book in the hope that her experience will be of use to other women. It is her gift. Elizabeth and I sat together one afternoon while she recounted her story.

Elizabeth: My experience of abortion is very different from yours, Isabella. I was married and had two children already. I just felt that I simply couldn't cope with another child at that stage. I thought I would go mad. My husband didn't understand but supported me in whatever decision I made. Now that I look back I wonder how I could have got into such a state about having a third child.

Not long ago I went to visit a friend who has two sons the same ages as mine. She has a younger child the same age as mine would have been. I was deeply upset by the experience of seeing her with her three children. I felt very depressed about it. My two sons played with her youngest child endlessly and it seemed that they would have loved having a younger brother or sister of their own. They aren't the sort of children who don't want any more children in the family. They have never asked for a baby or even mentioned one, but from their actions towards little children I know they would have accepted another child happily.

Isabella: And would you have another baby? Would you contemplate getting pregnant again?

Elizabeth: No! Never! I feel that I would be betraying the child I didn't have. I would be betraying that relationship. So I couldn't have another child — that's out of the question. Other people have asked me that too and my reply is always the same.

Isabella: You sound so certain. It's as if you still have some commitment to the child you didn't have. Almost as if that child is still around for you in a very real way. Is that so?

Elizabeth: I suppose so, yes. In a way I feel haunted by it all. By everything that I went through. It's good for me to talk about it all again, to reopen it all. A short while ago I thought I might be pregnant. My period was a day late. I was frantic. I went to have a coil fitted. The pain of having it fitted was excruciating. I didn't realise it would be so bad. But it was better than being pregnant. I spent the whole month with very bad pains and then I begged my GP to take it out. But the horror I felt at the thought that I might be pregnant was so intense, so vivid, that it made me realise, again, how far away I am from being healed of the wound of my abortion.

Isabella: Do you regret having an abortion?

Elizabeth: Yes, very much so. I wish I had known then what I know now. I wouldn't have done it.

Isabella: Would you tell your children that you have had an abortion?

Elizabeth: No, I wouldn't. The other morning while they were having breakfast my younger son asked us all, "What's an abortion?" My older son answered him, "It's when a mother kills the child that's growing inside her." I was shocked. How could I ever tell them that this is what I had done: 'killed the child growing inside me'? How could they begin to understand it? After all, I'm still married, happily married. There is no apparent reason why I couldn't have had another child. No, I couldn't tell them.

Isabella: I know that you have developed difficulties with your eyes, your sight, since the abortion and that you think this might have something to do with having had one.

Elizabeth: About a year after the abortion my eyesight started to get very bad and I was diagnosed as having a severe genetic disorder of my vision. I have been to so many people to see what could be done. Both my homoeopath and my osteopath feel that if only I could allow myself to see the face of my child then my eyes might start to improve. But I can't do that. The pain of seeing my child's face would be too intense, too overpowering. I just can't do it. I can't allow myself to see the child I might have had. The pain of it would be unbearable.

Isabella: More unbearable than what you have gone through already? More unbearable than what you are going through now?

Elizabeth: Yes, I think so. Or maybe I'm not ready for it. I've been told that it would be a good idea to write about my experience. But it's still so hazy. I know more or less when my abortion was. I'm not like you, Isabella, I don't remember when my baby would have been born. I don't have a clear picture of that. But I do know that at the same time every year I feel so depressed, unhappy and sad. Maybe if I let myself think about it, that's when my baby would have been born. But it's difficult to let myself think about it.

Isabella: It sounds to me as if this abortion has been a major turning point in your life, a catalyst of some sort. It's as if you have encountered life and death at a very deep level, in a very powerful way.

Elizabeth: I know that other people have planted a tree and done some sort of ritual in order to help them to heal. I haven't done any of that. It's as if something stops me and I don't know what that is. It doesn't have any meaning for me.

Isabella: Have you found anything that has meaning for you?

Elizabeth: Well, I think that everything to do with my eyes is very meaningful to me. After all, my sight is deteriorating and I'm a very visual person. I love colours. I love seeing my children, my house. Why should this have happened to me? No one in my family has this sight defect. They say it's genetic. Why should it have been triggered at this moment of my life? I think its meaning for me is that I am unable to let myself into the experience of seeing my baby. I feel that's something important and it's stopping me from healing myself. I know that my healing journey lies in my own hands. I know I can go to others for help, for support, but in the end it is up to me. No one else can do it for me. This is my pain, this is my journey.

Our conversation ended there. We agreed to meet again after the summer holidays. I typed this session up and sent it to Elizabeth to read. Two months later we met again:

Elizabeth: You know, it was so important for me to receive the transcript of our conversation. It was very important to see what I had actually said: what my words were as I spoke to you. Since our last meeting I have realised that I made the right decision to have an abortion. It was the right decision for me at the time. But everything has been connected to my vision. I have been thinking for 18 months that the initial diagnosis was a mistake, that the consultant had somehow made a mistake, but I know now that it's not a mistake. I realise that I had been hoping for a miracle. I had even thought that somebody would be clever enough to work it out but, as my sight is still deteriorating, I have come to the conclusion that my consultant was right. It is genetic and it is irreversible and as a result of separating my grief over my baby and my grief over my sight, which I have done since we last met, I can see now that he was right. I thought that having an abortion had affected my vision. That I had been responsible for what's happening. But I don't think my abortion made it happen. One event happened before the other. I don't think I created what's happening to me. Maybe what I am accepting is...

Elizabeth's voice trailed away. I watched her.

Elizabeth: I think what I'm accepting is that there's no link between my abortion and my sight. They were two separate events and when my homoeopath and my osteopath kept suggesting that if only I would allow myself to 'see' my child, then my vision would improve, I believed them and I linked the two events in my mind. But I *have* seen my child. I remember my child. For a month following the abortion until the birth time I was haunted physically and emotionally. I had numerous dreams about babies. And the ultimate dream was giving birth to a baby. It was unlike the two times that I have given birth before in that in my dream it was a completely painless experience.

I gave birth, in my dream, to a very tiny, white baby, completely white. I had never dreamt about babies before and haven't done so since. This is the only dream I have had where I gave birth. It's a dream I'll never forget for the rest of my life.

But I also gave birth to that baby in my life. I gave birth to it nine months later. It's you who made me realise. Do you remember? I felt really ill at that time and I hadn't thought about why I should be feeling so bad. It was you who asked me if it was the time that the baby would have been born. And then I realised it was!

And this time, this whole time from my abortion until after the 'birth' of my baby, was a time when I felt that nobody could understand what was happening to me. My husband was totally alien to the feelings I had and I resented the fact that he couldn't understand. Our relationship suffered. For me it was a time when I was in a bubble... where words couldn't express what was going on in my body. It was a terrible year. When I get into that state of grief I am completely disconnected from reality. I missed important appointments. I just forgot about them. I couldn't stand sex for a year and I wanted to be sterilised. I did the whole thing, went to my GP, made the appointment but then didn't turn up for the sterilisation. I had never had an anaesthetic before my abortion and I didn't want to put any more poison into my body. I felt that the anaesthetic was a poison.

My abortion has affected me in other ways, too. It has changed my view of what an abortion does to women and to those around them. It hasn't changed the fact that I still think that women should have a choice... I wouldn't campaign against abortion. But I realise that one can't go through an experience like that and remain unchanged.

I think I'm now able to see that two separate things happened to me. What's sad is that the grief for my eyes completely overshadowed my grief for the abortion and the one got confused with the other. This summer I have finally been able to grieve the abortion separately.

Isabella: I have a sense that over the summer you have come to some sort of resolution...

Elizabeth: And even as we're talking I have the feeling that separating the two issues may help my eyes too and maybe, at the same time, help me to come to terms with the loss of that baby. Doing this with you is helping me to do that. You know, Isabella, this is the first time I have talked about my abortion without crying.

MAGGIE'S STORY

For almost eighteen years I have lived with the nightmare of losing my child through abortion. For the majority of those years I denied to myself that I was deeply and irrevocably affected by that decision, a decision I made so long ago.

I went about my business as a caring child of ageing parents, caring sister, aunt, friend, teacher and counsellor. I'm good at what I do. I wore my mask with pride. I was fooling the world but no longer myself.

Today, as I write my story of healing as my contribution to Isabella's book, I'm in touch with the loss and pain that I believed I had dealt with. I planned today as a free day, to be by myself to accomplish this task. During the night I experienced low backache and stomach pains that ebbed and flowed with my breathing, the latter well practised through yoga and meditation. As light dawned around 5.30 am, I had a revelation. I had been in labour. Today I was going to give birth to my child. I had been given the opportunity to do it differently this second time round. I began to write...

And as I began to write to my child, now almost eighteen years old, the silent scream was with me once more.

Where are you now my wonderful child, my boy child? You were always a boy to me. I never wanted a girl. I wanted a boy with blond, curly hair like your father. Your father was well practised at being a dad. You had a brother and two sisters. But what you didn't have was a dad who was free to live with us and care for us as a family. However, your father loved you so very much that he wanted you to live, to have a life. I, for my own reasons, couldn't let you live.

You were inside my body for six weeks before I had them tear you out of me. The emotional and physical pain was excruciating. I was hurting and I wanted the world to know. "Hush," they said, "don't make so much noise. Think of all the other women. You will disturb them."

But I moaned and screamed even louder. You had gone from me. I had ended your life before it had hardly begun and they seriously expected me to 'hush'! I was told not to complain, that I had made a choice and I would have to live with the consequences of that. I was told that it wasn't OK to feel the loss of you and to grieve for you.

I felt as if they were telling me to deny my feelings in order to make everyone else happy. This attitude was familiar to me. Somewhere at the back of my consciousness was a memory of being little, of being in emotional pain, of being told that if I talked about how I was feeling I would upset everyone.

At first this memory was uncomfortable and disturbing but as it grew bigger in my awareness I recognised it as being comfortable after all, like an old overcoat. So I put on this old overcoat, I quietened down as they had requested and I went inside myself to that warm, dark place that was my core. I was at home in that place and nothing and nobody could harm me there. I had entered the home known as denial.

I told your father and my boss that I was OK. It was nothing. The decision to terminate your life was the right one and now I could get on with my life. I LIED. Oh, how I lied! I was beside myself. Inside I was screaming, screaming, screaming, flailing unseen arms to reach out to anyone who would recognise my pain and hold me while I struggled to live through this waking nightmare.

Eventually my screams subsided. I whimpered for what seemed an eternity. Nobody noticed. I whimpered, swallowed, ate what was put in front of me, swallowed and whimpered. I laughed with the other women about the woman who had been screaming. I entered a world where I became two people: One who didn't show any reaction to the abortion and the other who lived in the deep shadows, terrified of being discovered.

I colluded in keeping a secret. My guilt, shame and loss were immense but not open for acknowledgement, not even with your father. I felt bereft and totally alone. I felt that no one could possibly understand me and not judge me. I didn't understand myself and I was primitive in my self-judgement. Even to begin to understand me at this point, my child, you have to know other things about me:

During my ten years of marriage I had been investigated for infertility. Nothing was found to be wrong with me once a blocked tube had been successfully unblocked. All I had ever wanted was children. I worked with children. I saw myself as an earth mother type.

Imagine then my shock when, within three months of the breakdown of my marriage, I found I was pregnant. I was pregnant by my lover, your father. From the first day of my missed period I knew I was pregnant and I also knew, inexplicably, that I wouldn't be having this child. This child that was you, that is you.

I had no money, I had just begun social work training and I had nowhere to live. Your father would have supported us financially but wouldn't have been able to acknowledge us publicly.

At this time I had a recurring vision of you and me walking down the street. On the other side of the street your father was walking with his other family. You weren't aware of them and I couldn't tell you who they were.

Although I didn't believe in abortion I decided that the only course of action open to me was to have one. If I couldn't give you a father, then I couldn't give you a life at all. This experience of flying in the face of my deeply held values taught me about the acceptance that comes through being non-judgemental. From that day to this I believe I have attempted to have a more accepting view of others.

However, until three years ago I had been totally unaccepting of myself. Following a hysterectomy — you would have been six years old at the time — I was told that conceiving a child had not been a problem for me. The problem was carrying a child. I had had the abortion unnecessarily. My insides were so diseased that it was more than likely I would have spontaneously aborted you anyway.

The anger I felt towards my body was added to the guilt and shame I already felt and I pushed them all down deeper into the dark secret core of me. I worked and played harder than ever. I became even more successful in my career and was even proud of my ability to return to work only six weeks following surgery!

So you are probably wondering what happened three years ago. You would have been fifteen by then. I was in training to become a counsellor and I got in touch again with the pain so successfully hidden for so long. As a result, I quietly shared my experience with Isabella. I had never told another living soul apart from your father and my boss.

Her acceptance of me was the release that I needed to begin my healing. I began the enormously painful task of examining myself and learning to accept myself. Most of this work took place with my counsellor but gradually I began to share my experience with my close female friends. I was terrified that I was risking too much: their friendship, their acceptance of me, their anger and their judgement.

But to my astonishment I was accepted! They shared their own experiences of abortion with me. I couldn't tell which of them was in the 'abortion club' and of course they couldn't know that I was in it either. The relief of not being alone with my experience and my pain was like a dam bursting. Suddenly I was able to talk about it quite freely and to be more accepting of myself.

Through the talking, the crying, the laughing and the acceptance, the real healing took place. I was able to look at children of all ages without feeling pain in my heart. My friends who were coming to the grandmother stage of their lives began to feel freer about sharing their happy news. I welcomed this gladly. I didn't want to feel that I existed in a twilight world where children were a taboo subject.

Of course, I felt regret and envy that I was never going to

be a grandmother but I could now share their delight. This time around I didn't deny my feelings; I shared them and cried for the loss of you, alone and with my friends.

Last year I spent three months in Spain working at an alternative holiday centre. While I was there, your seventeenth birthday came around. As part of my healing and reconciliation with your spirit, I planted an ebullient red-flamed hibiscus in a warm, sunny spot. The young plant grows in the shelter of an older hibiscus where I feel that he can grow and flourish in the world. As a summer baby I assumed that you, the red-flamed hibiscus, would be at your happiest in the sun. I lit a candle and marked your birth in quiet meditation. I felt almost at peace. I say almost because I was aware that there was still something missing from my healing journey.

In May of this year Isabella approached me with a request to contribute my story to this book. I was honoured to have been asked but totally unprepared for my reaction. I was thrown into emotional turmoil. I relived the abortion over and over again. Night and day I found no peace. I talked it over at length with my counsellor and made a decision that writing my story would assist me in my healing.

A short while later I returned to Spain. I visited you, the red-flamed hibiscus. You had grown so strong and tall that I hardly recognised you. The visit was both a painful and a happy experience. I realised that by writing my story I was being given a second chance to give birth to you. I could let you out into the world with pride. I would be leaving something of myself in the world after all. My life wouldn't have been in vain and yours wouldn't have been either.

You are about to be eighteen years old, my son, a man in the eyes of the world. It's time for you to leave me and go out into the world to find yourself. I let you go with love, so much love, and with pride. You have taught me so much and for that I shall always be humble and grateful.

MEDICAL MARRIAGE

The New Partnership between Orthodox and Complementary Medicine

※ A model for health care in the 21st century
※ Comprehensive information on 63 complementary therapies
※ Thought provoking essays to catalyse change

by Dr Cornelia Featherstone and Lori Forsyth

Written, compiled and edited by a medical doctor and a complementary practitioner, this book is an excellent example of co-operation. It epitomises the synergy which occurs when the two paradigms – the reductionist and the holistic – meet in mutual respect and open-mindedness: common ground is found and integrated health care becomes reality.

Patients are leading the way, as they are already making use of both complementary and orthodox medicine to increase their health care options. It is time for health care professionals in both fields to acknowledge each other's contributions and offer patients the quality of care which is only achievable through united and concerted action.

This book is essential reading for everyone interested in the field of health care. Doctors, nurses and complementary practitioners will find a wealth of information enabling them to work in multidisciplinary co-operation. Patients and conscious consumers will gain insight into the possibilities of integrated health care, allowing them to make educated choices about their own care.

Paperback 640 pages • ISBN 1 899171 16 9 • £19.95 • US$29.95 • CAN$39.95
Available from all good bookshops, or direct from
Findhorn Press for £19.95 including p&p

This is a warm, wonderful, thorough and above all honest exploration of a new medical dimension which is emerging out of mutually respectful teamwork between orthodox and complementary health care professionals... The messages which this book offers should be read – and above all applied – by every health care professional.

— Leon Chaitow ND DO
Consultant osteopath and naturopath
Marylebone Health Centre (NHS), London

...it is important that patients do take responsibility for their own health and furthermore it is important that doctors adopt a more co-operative and less pedagogic attitude to their patients and health care in general... so much of the book is excellent common sense, clearly written and a superb blueprint for the future.

— Dr G T Lewith MA DM MRCP MRCGP
Honorary Visiting Clinical Senior Lecturer
Southampton University

HOLISTIC MENOPAUSE
Judy Hall

Holistic Menopause offers women positive, natural choices. It acknowledges the existence of all levels of being: body, mind and spirit. It asks you to listen to your own intuition, to empower yourself and take charge of your own life. Menopause can be a time of honouring and releasing all that has gone before, of realising that each moment of life can be a celebration, and that there are infinite possibilities for growth. Using this book may totally change the way you live, helping you to see that this can be the best time of your life and that it can only get better.

£9.95/US$15.95 pbk 272 pages • ISBN 1 899171 32 0

THE ART OF PSYCHIC PROTECTION
Judy Hall

A book of practical techniques and help for any individual or group seeking to expand their consciousness who need to protect themselves from psychic intrusion. For those who meditate, use guided imagery or self-hypnosis tapes, for therapists and healers, for those who find excessive tiredness a problem, the chances are that these people need to protect themselves with these tried and tested tools, some of which date back thousands of years whilst others belong to the 21st century. We protect ourselves in so many ways, we have tended to forget that psychic protection is a basic need.

£5.95 Pbk 144 pages • ISBN 1 899171 36 3

FINDHORN FLOWER ESSENCES
Marion Leigh

Marion explains the theory, preparation and practical applications of the flower essences. The book also includes a thorough, indexed repertoire of illnesses and their indicated treatments.

£9.95/US$16.95 pbk 121 pages
ISBN 1 899171 96 7

AMAZONIAN GEM & ORCHID ESSENCES
Andreas Korte, Antje & Helmut Hofmann

The vibratory qualities of Amazonian gems and orchids have been extracted for their therapeutic effects. This book describes each of the essences and its applications.

£9.95/US$16.95 pbk 116 pages
(inc. 40 detachable colour cards)
ISBN 1 899171 91 6

AUSTRALIAN BUSH FLOWER ESSENCES
Ian White

An informative yet personal picture of fifty bush flower essences and detailed information about their preparation and use in all areas of healing. Fully Illustrated. The Australian Bush Flower Essences themselves are available in the UK and many other countries.

£11.95/US$19.95 pbk 210 pages (16 in colour)
ISBN 0 905249 84 4